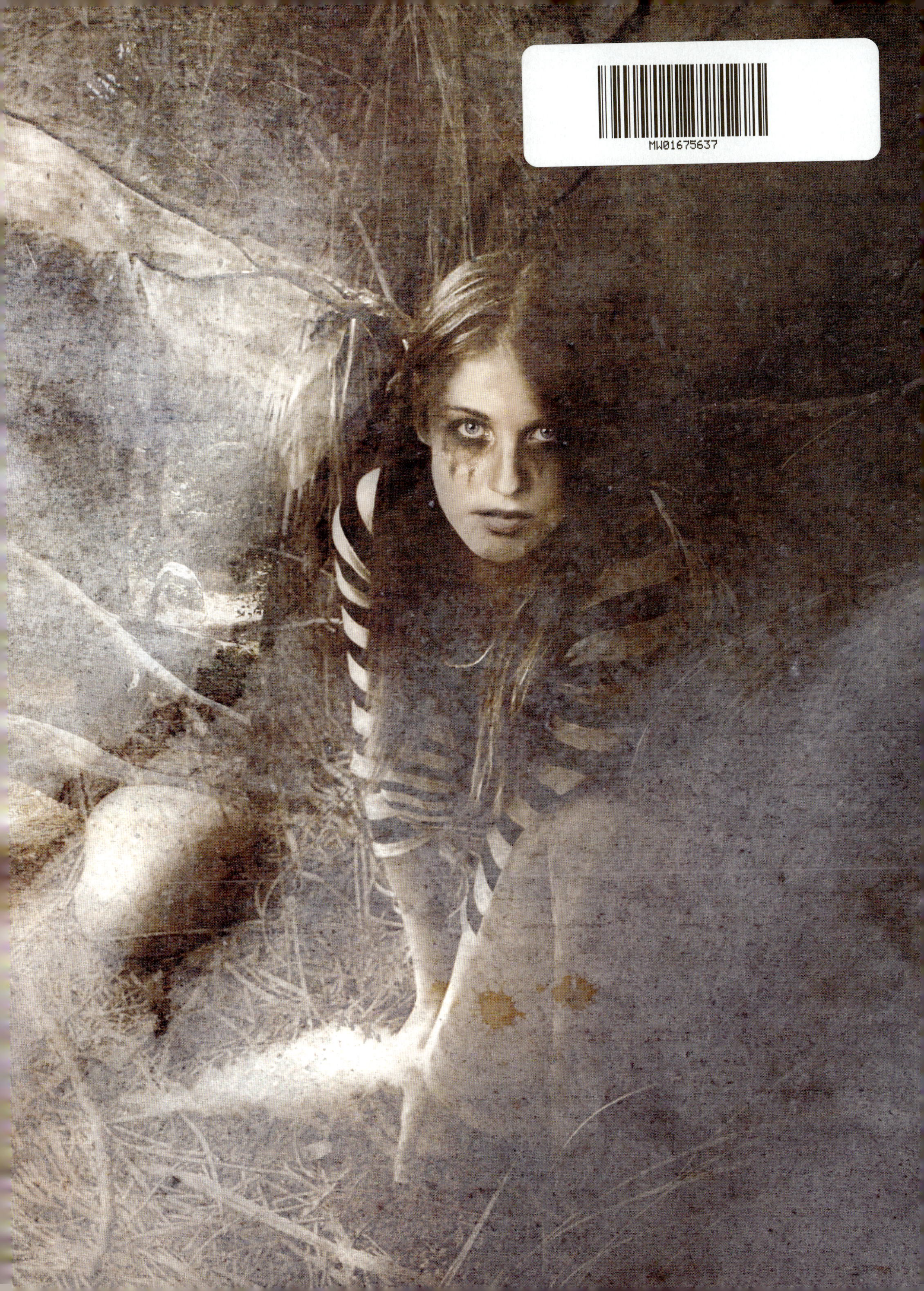

MW01675637

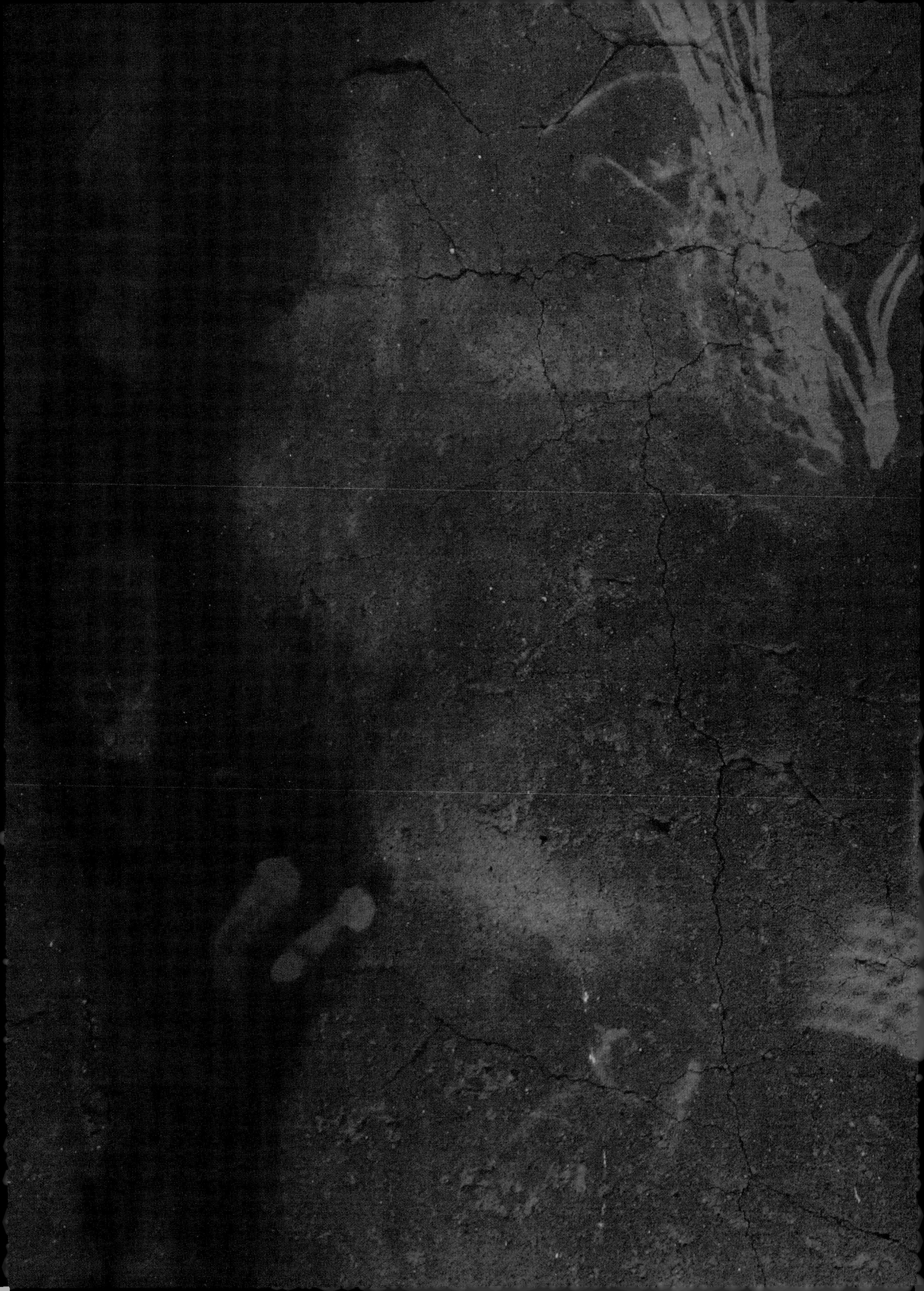

J. CORSENTINO'S

TIME of the FAERIES

Cover Design: Stephanie Lostimolo
Graphic Design: Joseph Corsentino, Stephanie Lostimolo
Art Direction: Robert Gould
Editing: Nancy Berman

Library of Congress Cataloging-in-Publication Data has been applied for.
ISBN: 0-9779956-2-3

Design and Compilation © 2007 Imaginosis
Text and Artwork © 2007 Joseph Corsentino

All rights reserved. Published by Imaginosis.
No part of this publication may be reproduced, stored in a retrieval system, or transmitted in any form or by any means, electronic, mechanical, photocopying, recording, or otherwise, without prior written permission of the publisher.

Printed in China by Regent Publishing Services Limited.
10 9 8 7 6 5 4 3 2 1

An IMAGINOSIS Book

Please visit the official Time of the Faeries website:
timeofthefaeries.com

IMAGINOSIS
A TRANSMEDIA ARTS COMPANY
4195 Crisp Canyon
Sherman Oaks, CA 91403
Imaginosis.com

J. CORSENTINO'S

TIME of thE FAERIES

IMAGINOSIS
LOS ANGELES

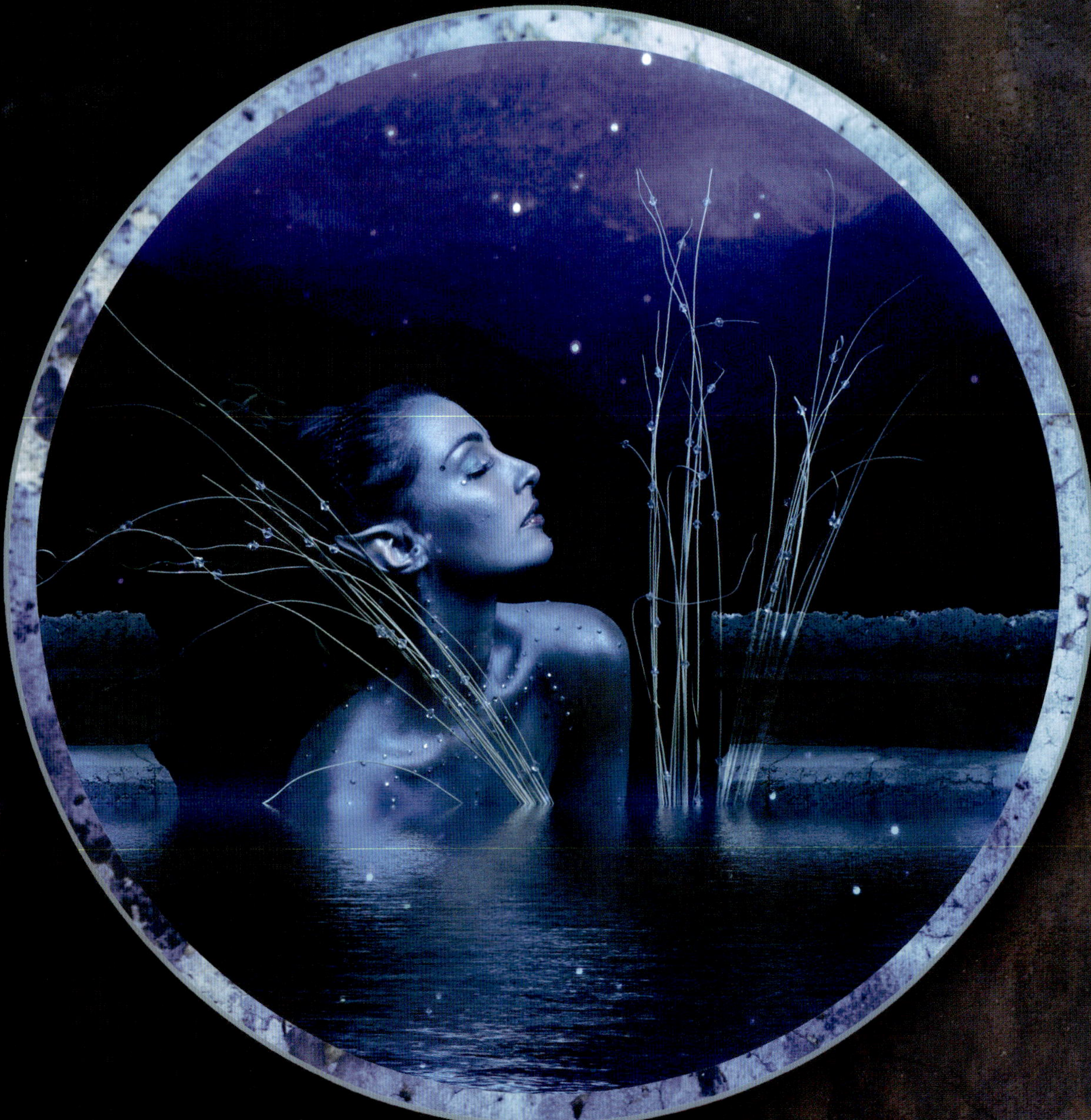

INTRODUCTION

For me, photography has always been about capturing light and shadow but it's a Magick that I almost didn't experience. Thanks to one of the catalytic moments when life is leading you in one direction and some unexpected, random element crosses your path that to your amazement pays off years later, I am a photographer today. When that moment arrived, I was already gathering friends to play dress-up and directing shoots involving strange tales of science fiction and fantasy. Fun, stimulating, but it made me want to know more, to do more and photography opened a world to me.

A project I had been working on for years fell through and I found myself facing a dark time. Again, the unexpected moment occurred: "someone" flew into my life, ignited a spark, and after a series of beautiful moments, flew out again. It was from that encounter that the idea to re-invent faerie lore in a modern setting began to burn inside me. "What would happen if faeries returned into the modern world?" I asked myself. "How would they be welcomed? How would they hide or blend in? What kind of trouble would they get themselves into? How would they affect us in our concrete jungles, so alien from their ancient forested ones?"

To realize what I was seeing in my mind and feeling in my heart, I knew something more than pictures would be required. I remembered when faeries and angels were painted as reflection of the times and as artistic metaphors: I wanted to approach my concept in the same spirit. In this way, a simple pictorial idea of photographing faeries turned into an entire world that became very real to me.

I found my muses in the friends I had when I first started shooting and in random people with whom I shared brief moments during paradigm shifts of my life. The pictures became a conversation, a dialog in image, often engaged in late at night after too many drinks when the world seemed rich, dark and filled with magick.

I sought to capture these moments after dark and the colorful people who populate the night, each one a chaotic collection of particles of possibility holding a serendipitous sway on everyday life. These night-enchanted beings, denizens of both modern cities and ancient forests, became my faeries and I began to unwind their noir tales using light, shadow, images and ink.

The tale of fiction I tell here is about us: who we are, how we relate and most important, how we deal with the latent magickal talents we all have within us. These are tales of inspiration that inspire and provoke. They are stories of causality and responsibility; of faith and courage; of synchronicity and circumstance. All the magickal beings of my world: the Faeries, Angels, Darklings, Nephilim, & Shadme are metaphors for the greater forces that move and transform our lives.

So here is the beginning, a history, a prologue of sorts, with hopes that it will lead us to various doors, windows, keyholes, questions, thoughts, through which, in days to come, the tales of The Time of The Faeries will further unfold.

Please enjoy,
Joseph Corsentino

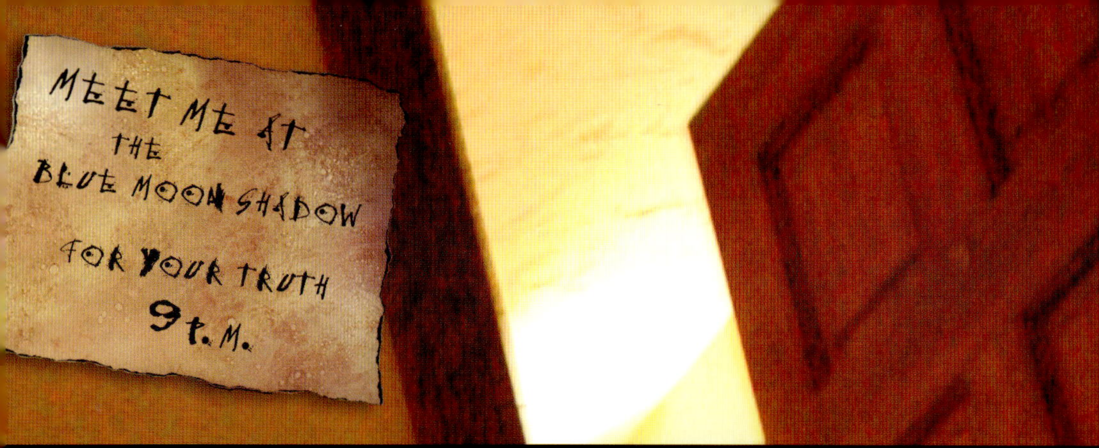

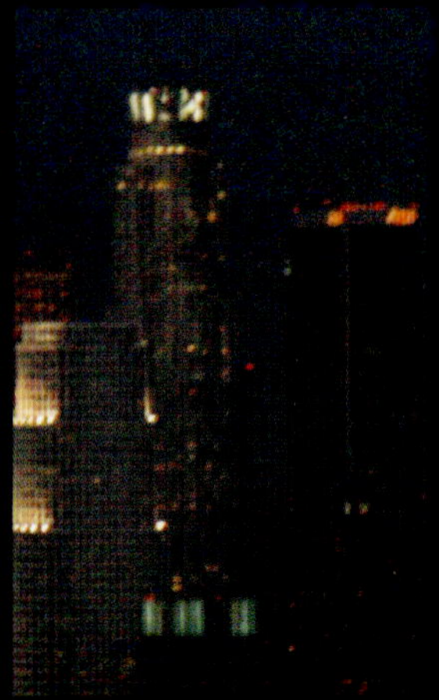

EVERYONE IS MOVING.

Through smoke, machines, sound, bodies. All in a hurry, oblivious, rushing through civil insanity to get somewhere that they think is important. I watch them from the bar; watch and learn. I watch to distract myself so I do not become one of them. I watch and wait. For hours. This better be worth it, for damn sure. I finished my drink and got up and suddenly there he was, his eyes friendly, welcoming, old.

"Hello Emily." He smiled and sat down.

"You're late."

"Actually, you were early."

"You said 9 PM."

"Yes, but I was in a different time zone when I said it." He snapped open an old pocket watch: 9 PM.

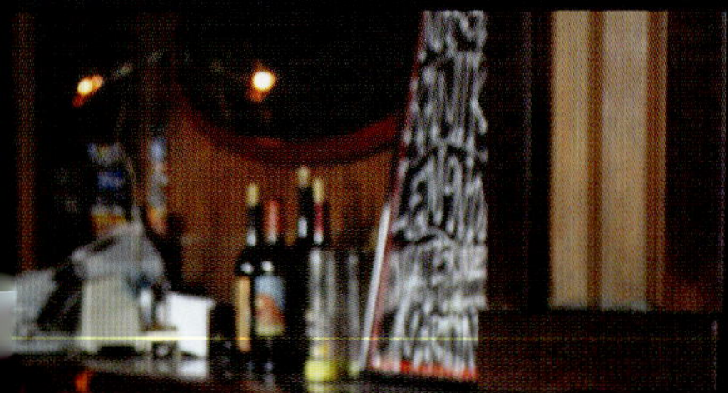

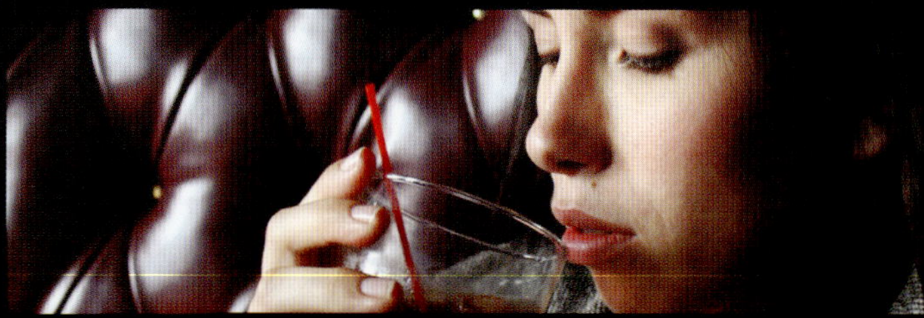

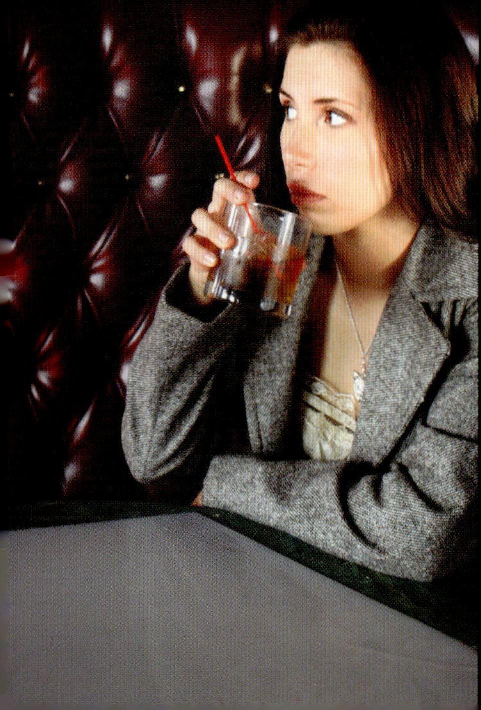

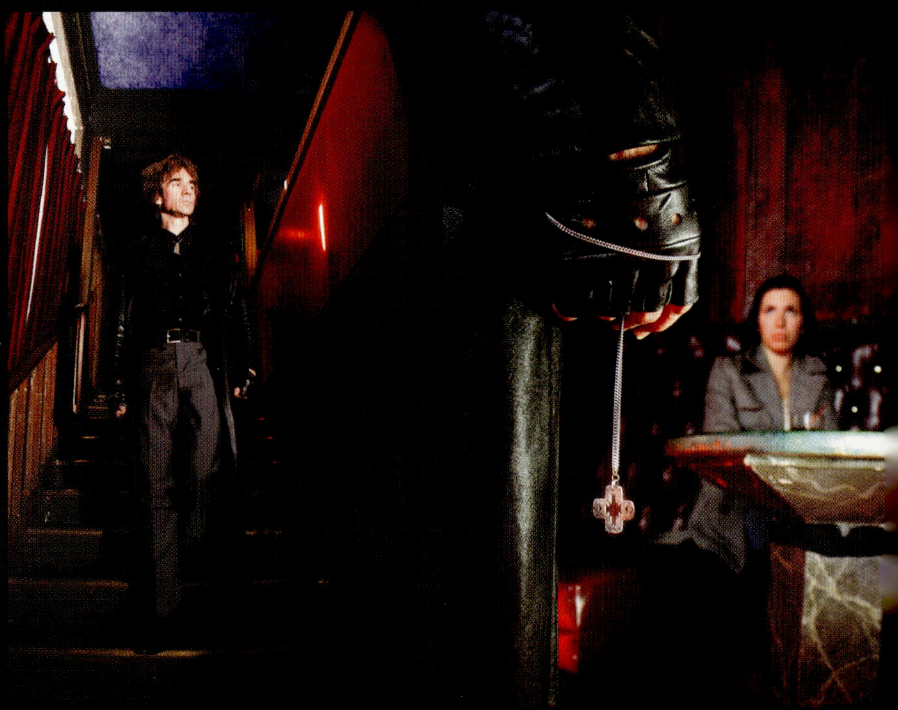

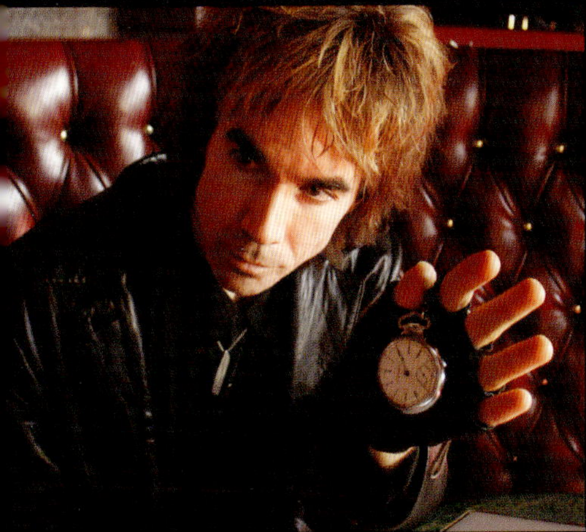

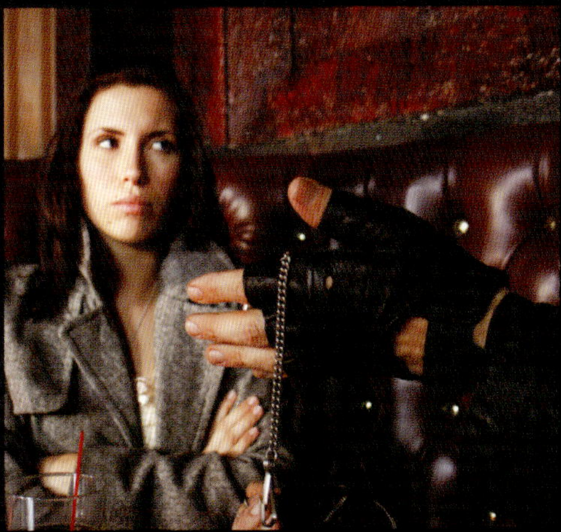

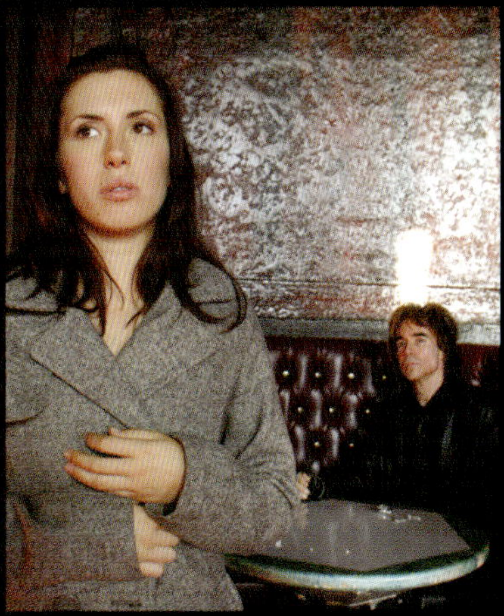

I started to move away. "I don't have time for this…"

"Considering your unique dilemma Ms. Evans, you don't have time *not* to hear this."

Intrigued, I sat back down and met his confident gaze.

"Don't be nervous; I won't bite," he laughed.

I felt myself relax. "So you'll tell me what I need to know?"

He touched my hand, lightly, for a moment. "The truth? Of course, but…"

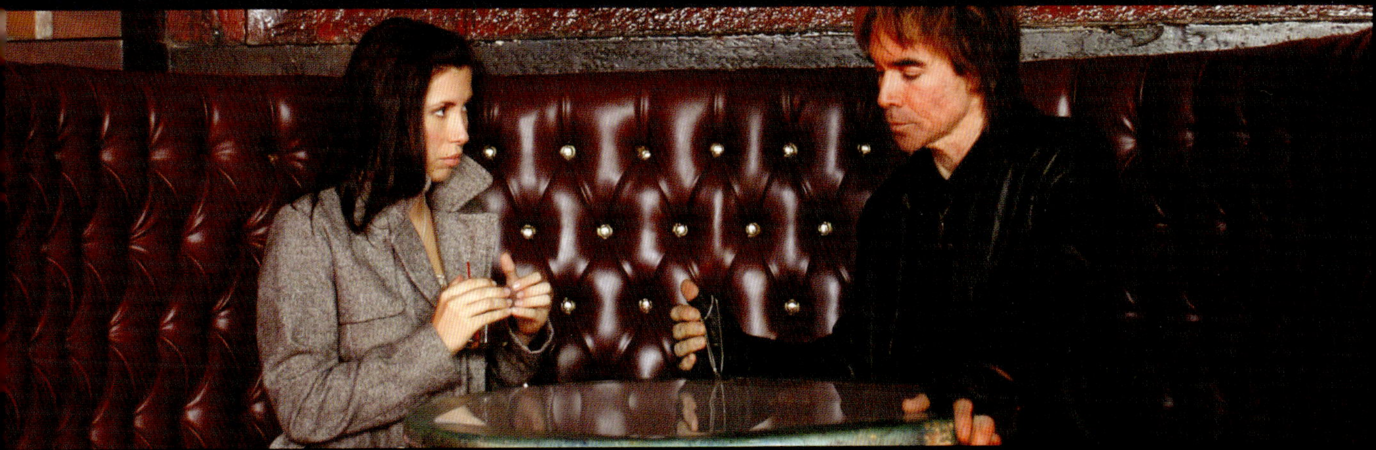

"See, there is always a 'but'."

"Yes... always. Ms. Evans, I will tell you everything you want to know... for a price. Don't be afraid; it's a small thing, easily given. Might even help you. So, your choice: answers or ignorance – what's your pleasure?"

Weird as this all was, I had to know what was happening to me. I wanted answers. For no reasonable reason, I trusted him. "Agreed."

He closed his eyes and smiled. "Done."

And he leaned forward, looking so deep
into my eyes that I fell into their liquid light and heard within
my heart and soul a voice that said:

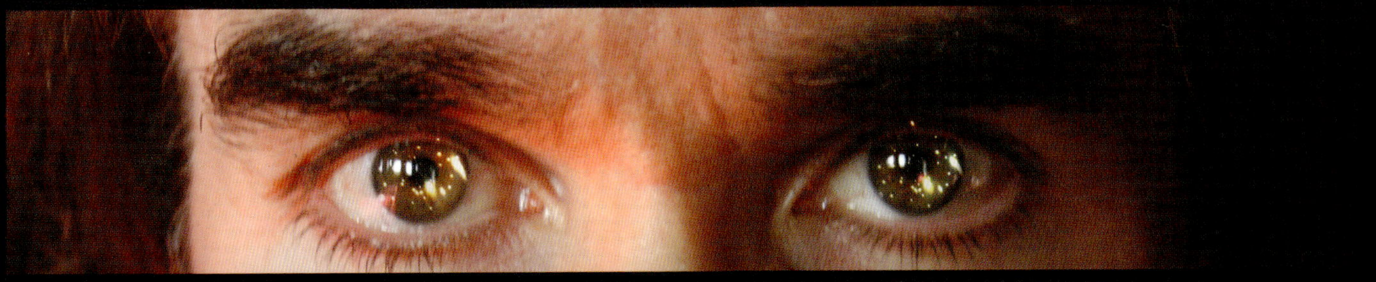

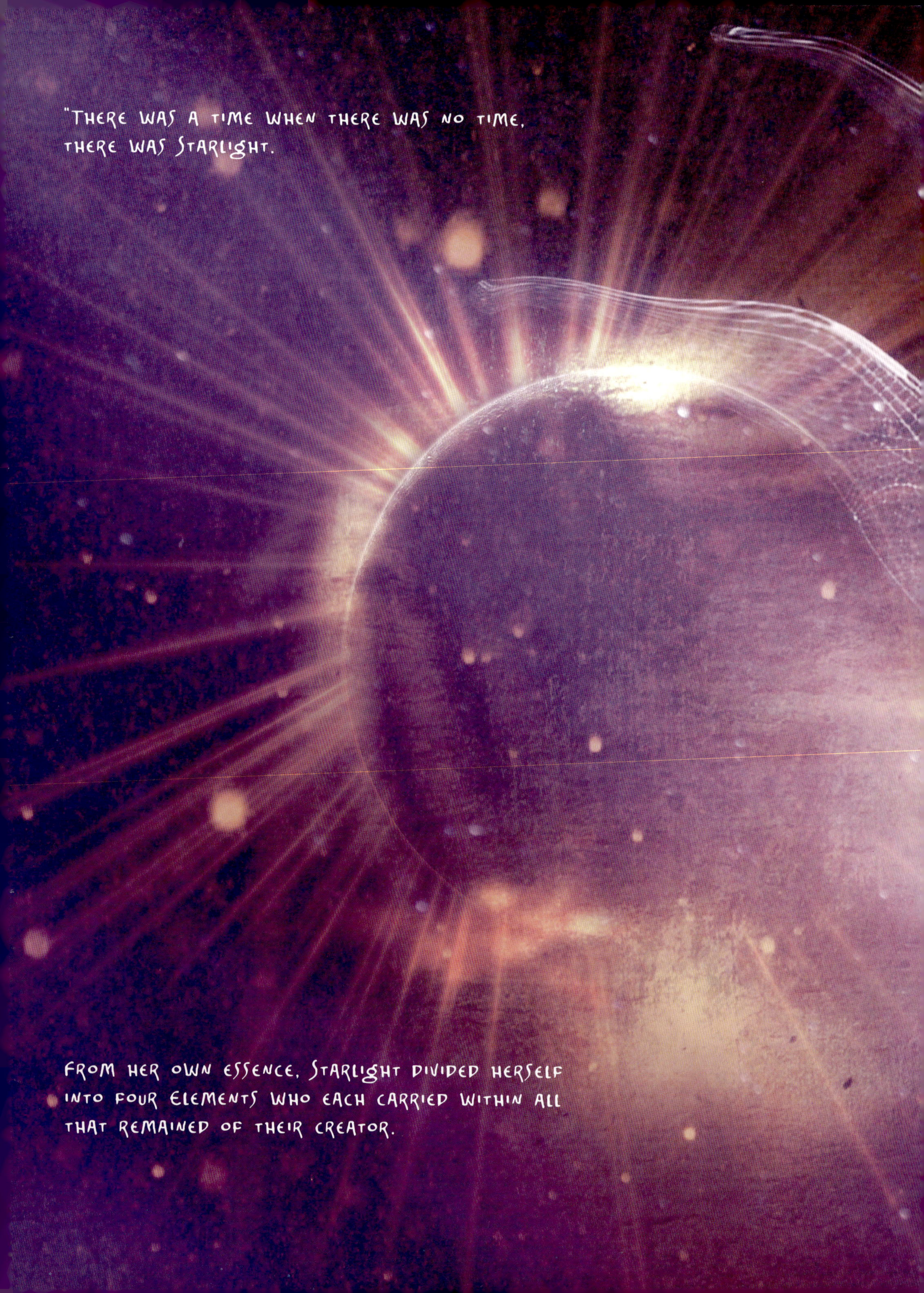
"There was a time when there was no time. there was Starlight.
From her own essence, Starlight divided herself into four Elements who each carried within all that remained of their creator.

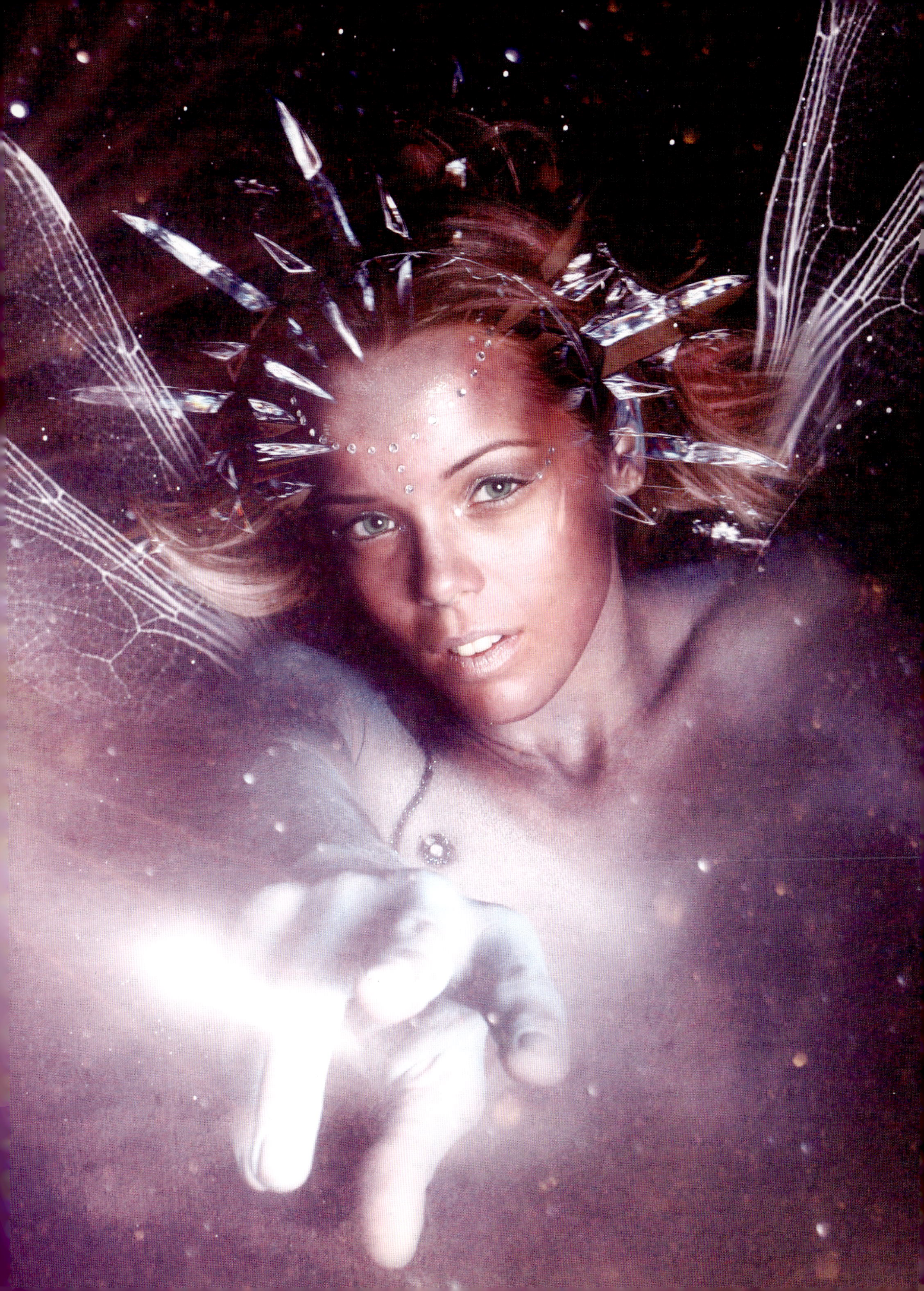

The Elementals were pure, natural forms of beatific energy and in time they gave themselves shape, substance, and identity: Earith, the Earth Elemental; Syon, the Water Elemental; Aidrilae, the Air Elemental; and Cendri, the Fire Elemental.

It was their forms that brought forth the magickal creatures we know today as faeries.

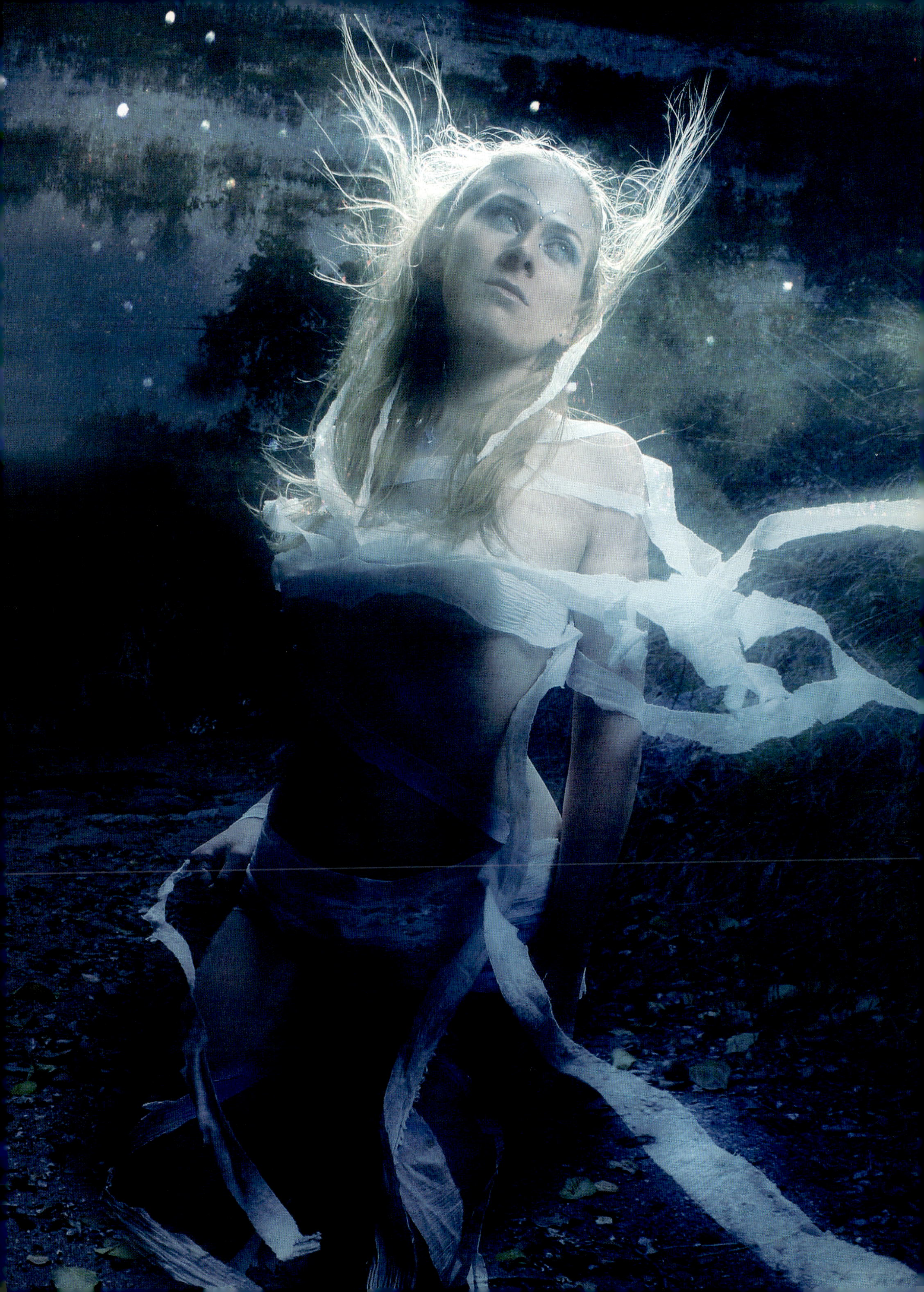

THE FAERIES THRIVED IN THE FORESTS, WATERS, MOUNTAINS AND OPEN PLAINS OF OUR WORLD. THEY LIKED TO WATCH HUMANS AND TEASE THEM JUST BECAUSE THEY COULD.

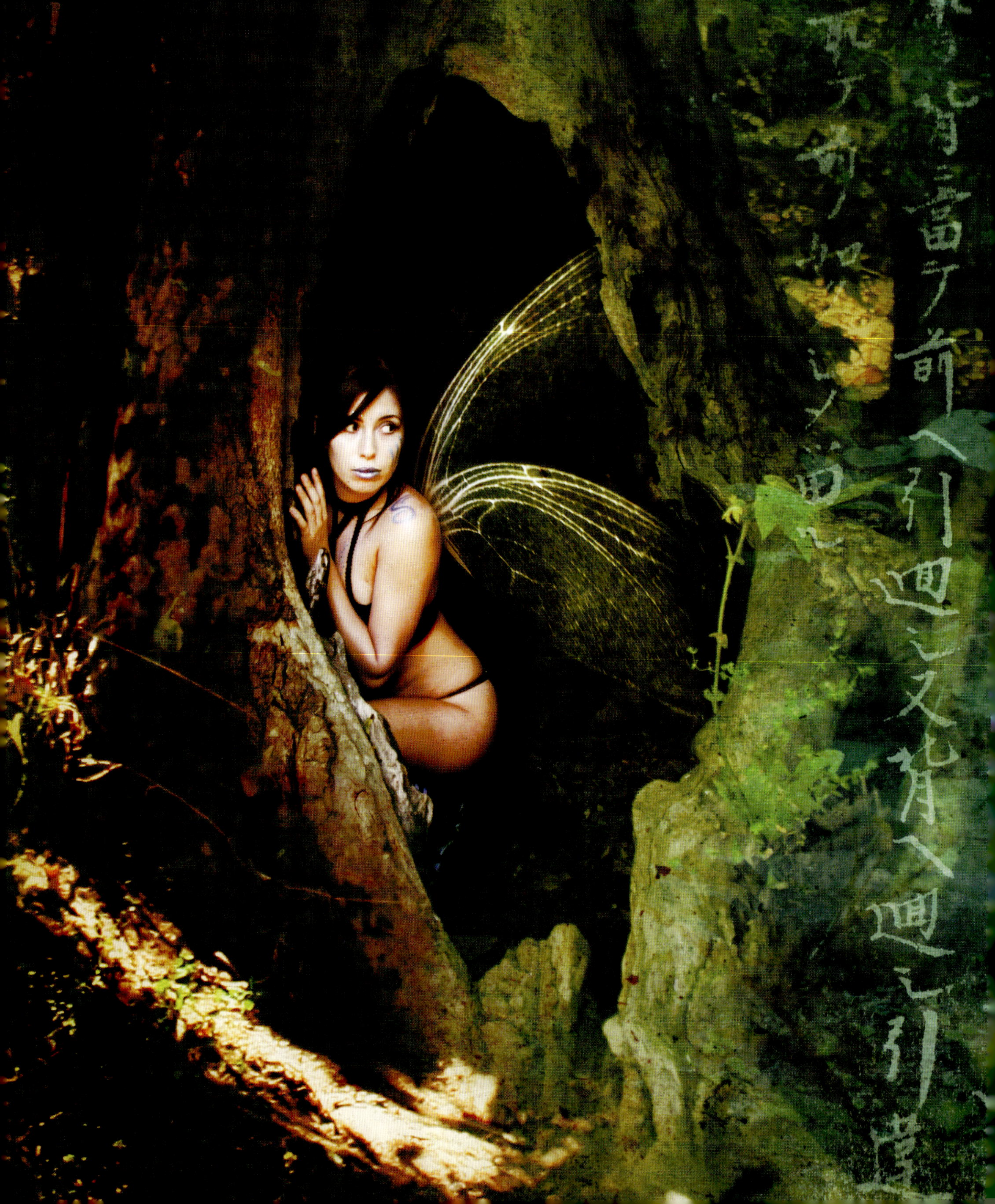

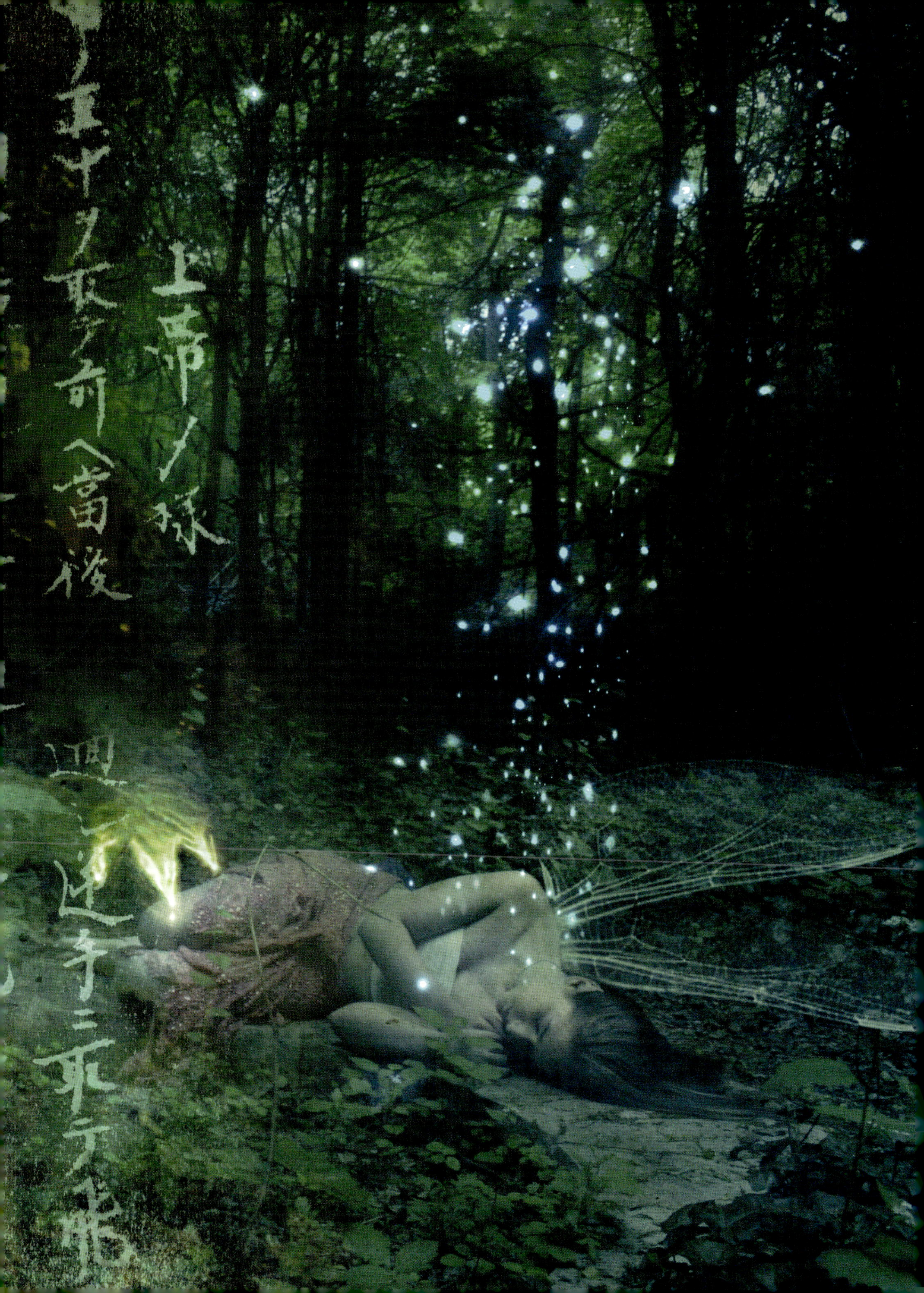

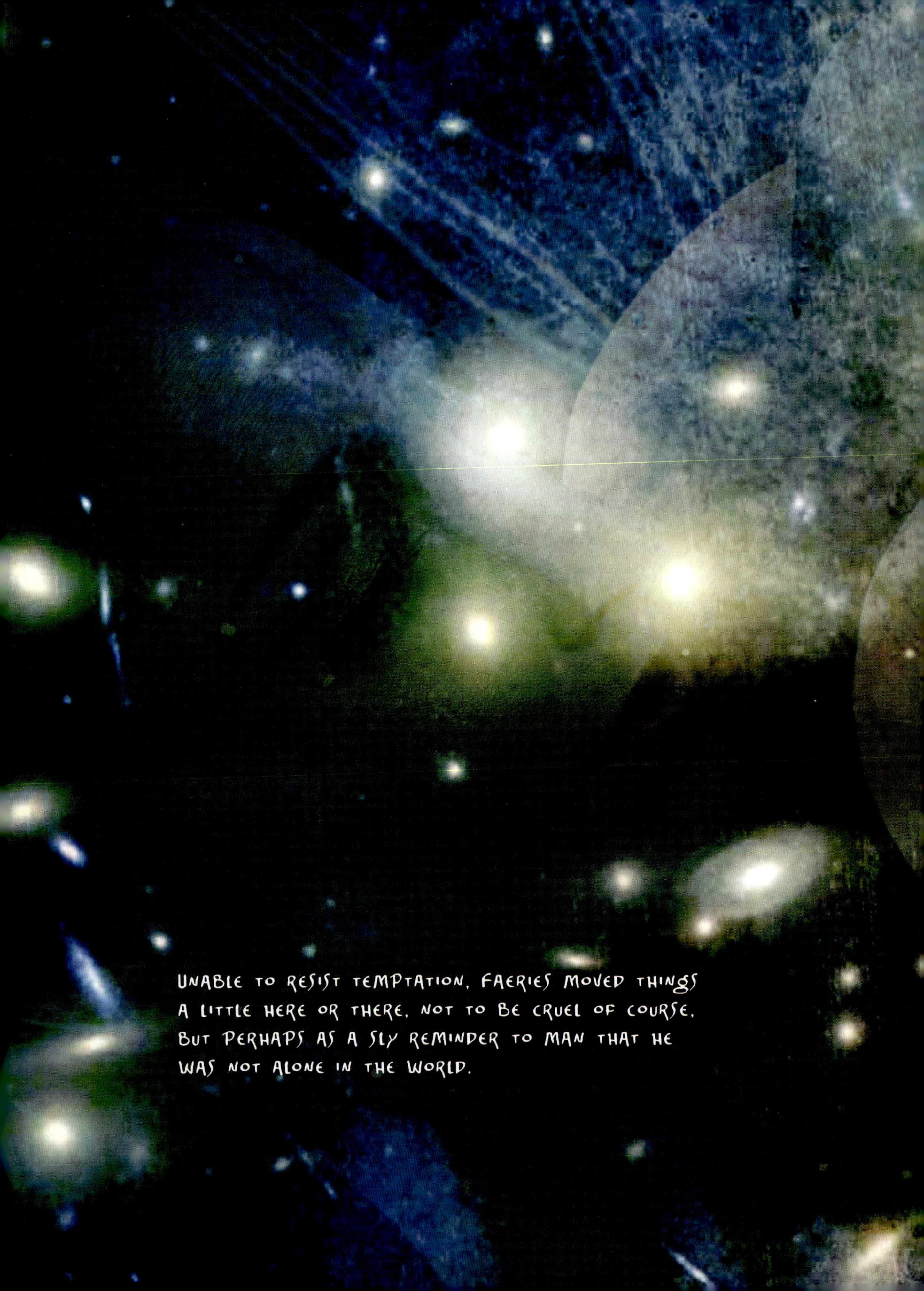

UNABLE TO RESIST TEMPTATION, FAERIES MOVED THINGS A LITTLE HERE OR THERE, NOT TO BE CRUEL OF COURSE, BUT PERHAPS AS A SLY REMINDER TO MAN THAT HE WAS NOT ALONE IN THE WORLD.

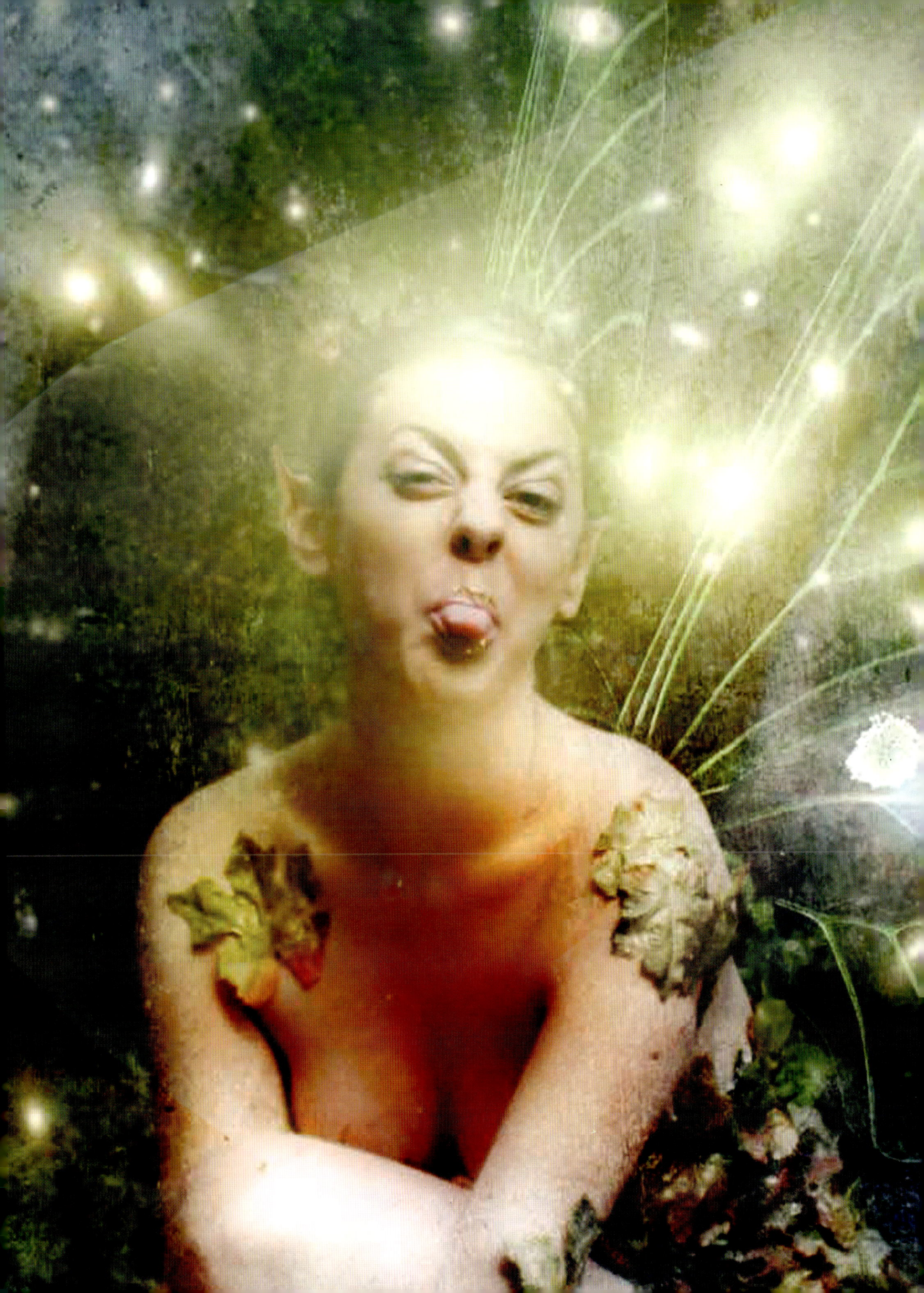

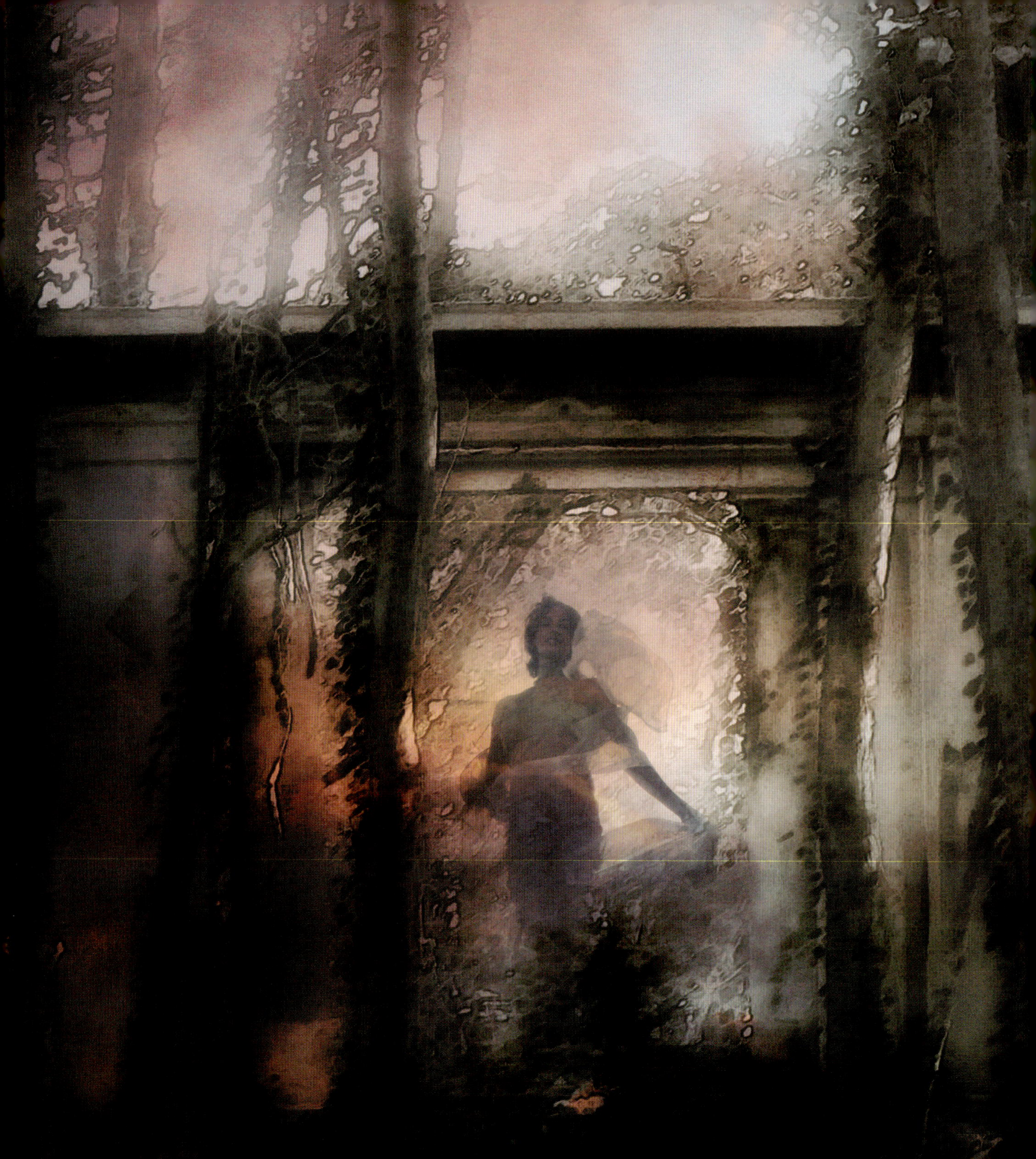

THERE WAS EVEN A TIME WHEN FAERIE AND HUMAN LIVED TOGETHER IN HARMONY. A COURT OF MAGICK WAS FORMED IN THE KINGDOMS OF MEN TO COMMUNE WITH THE REALM.

AND FOR A TIME, THINGS WERE GOOD.

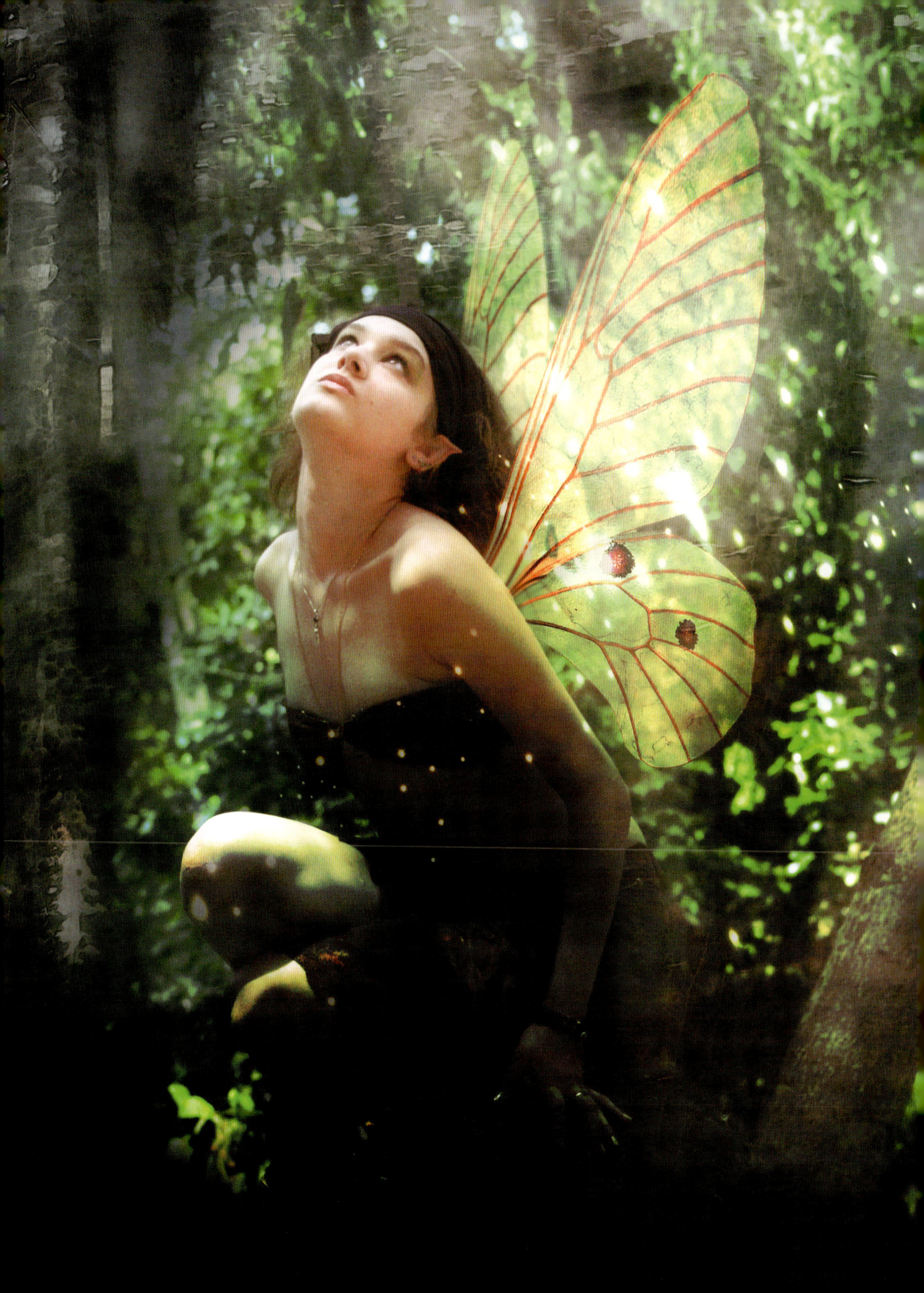

But as they say, all good things must come to an end.

One dark day the powerful Queen of the Faeries went mad, and in a single moment, a tragic misunderstanding born of blind rage shattered the peace and doomed the world to battle. Losses to both sides were beyond counting and neither side emerged

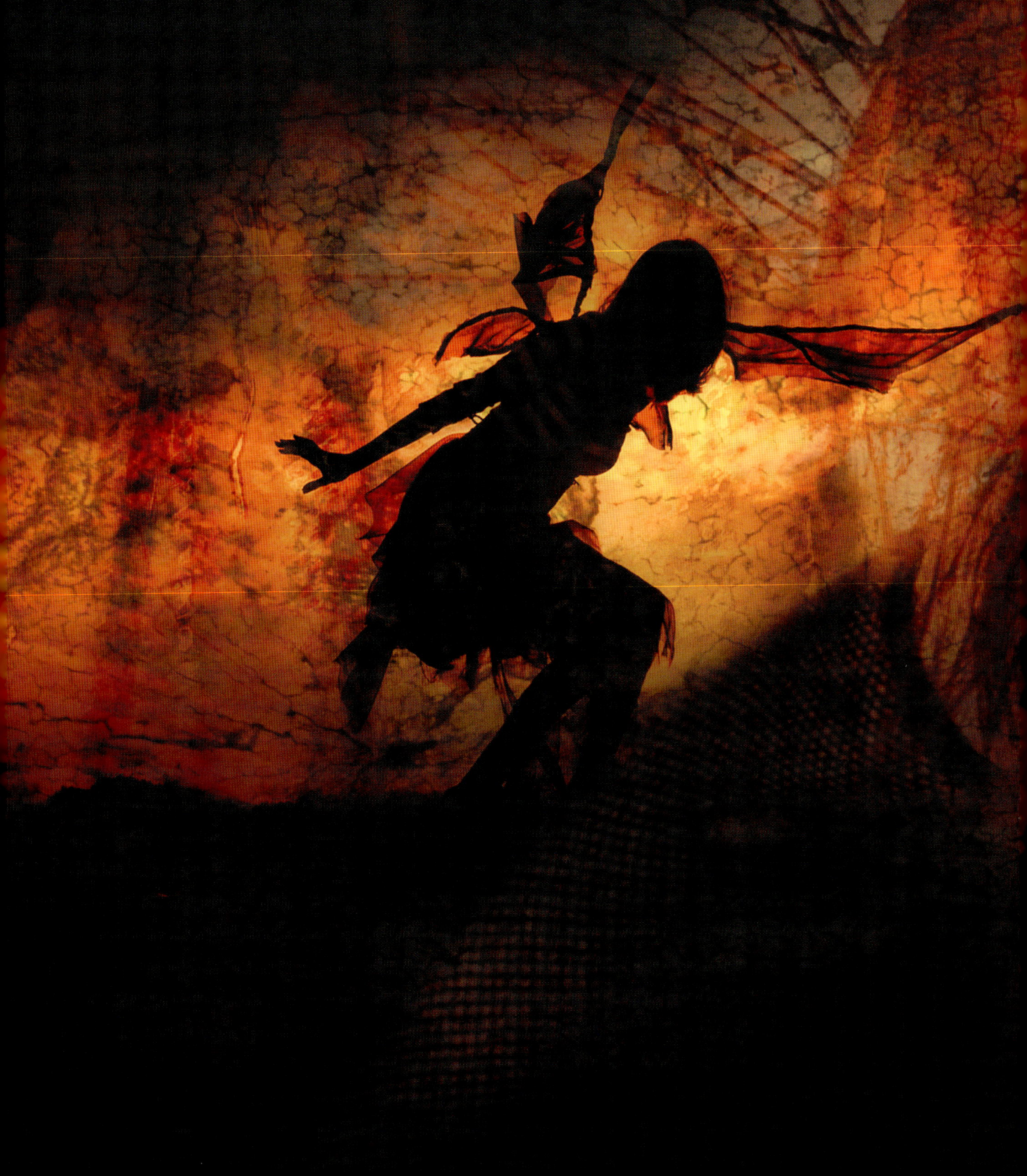

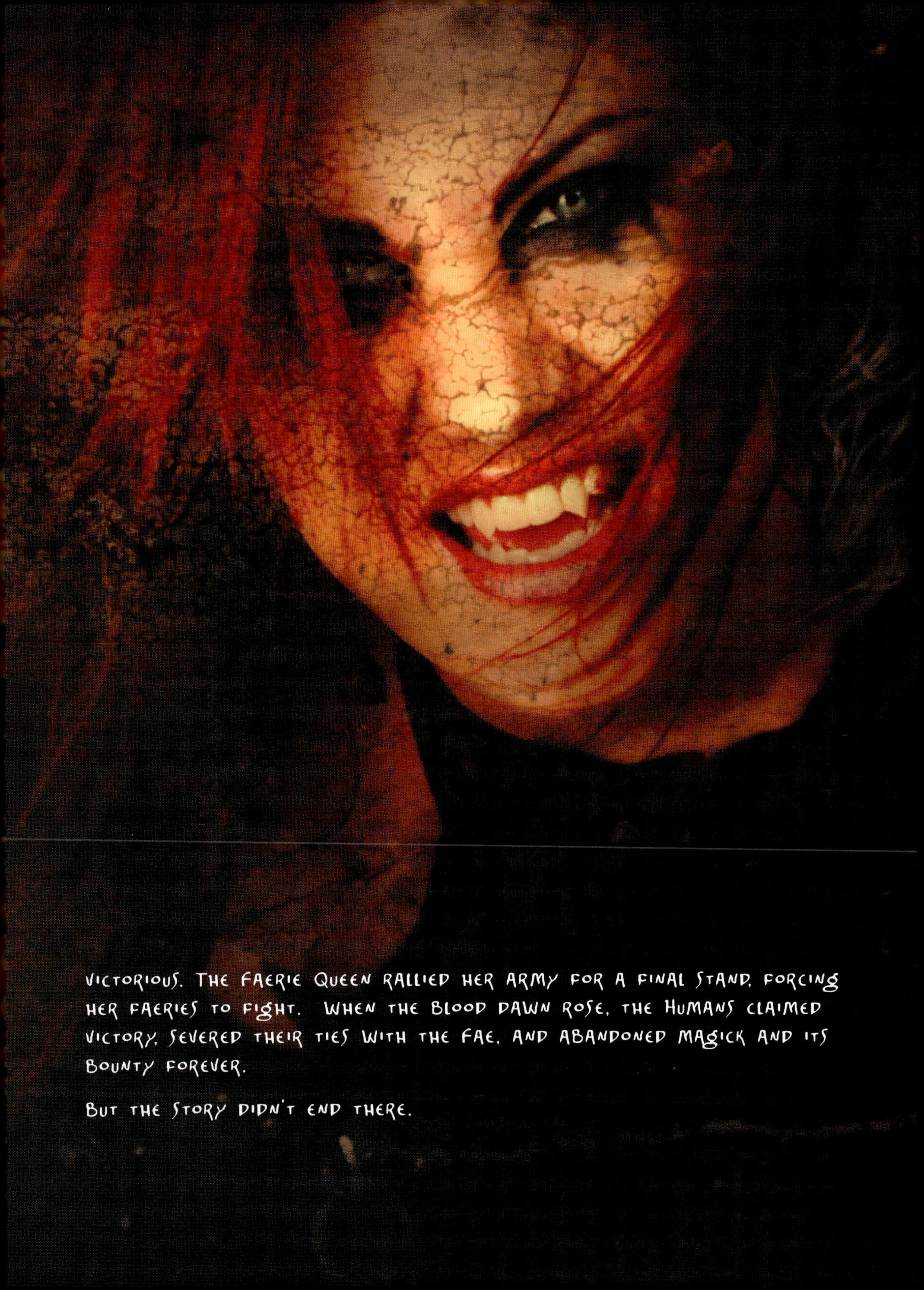

Victorious. The Faerie Queen rallied her army for a final stand, forcing her faeries to fight. When the Blood Dawn rose, the Humans claimed victory, severed their ties with the Fae, and abandoned Magick and its bounty forever.

But the story didn't end there.

Horrified by the violence and devastation to their beautiful world, some faeries retreated into Twilight, the far lands protected by barriers of light and shadow that kept their realm safe from those who would hunt and destroy them. After a time, many faeries swore never to trust the ways of men again and soon forgot about the human world which held a heart cold to the spark of magick.

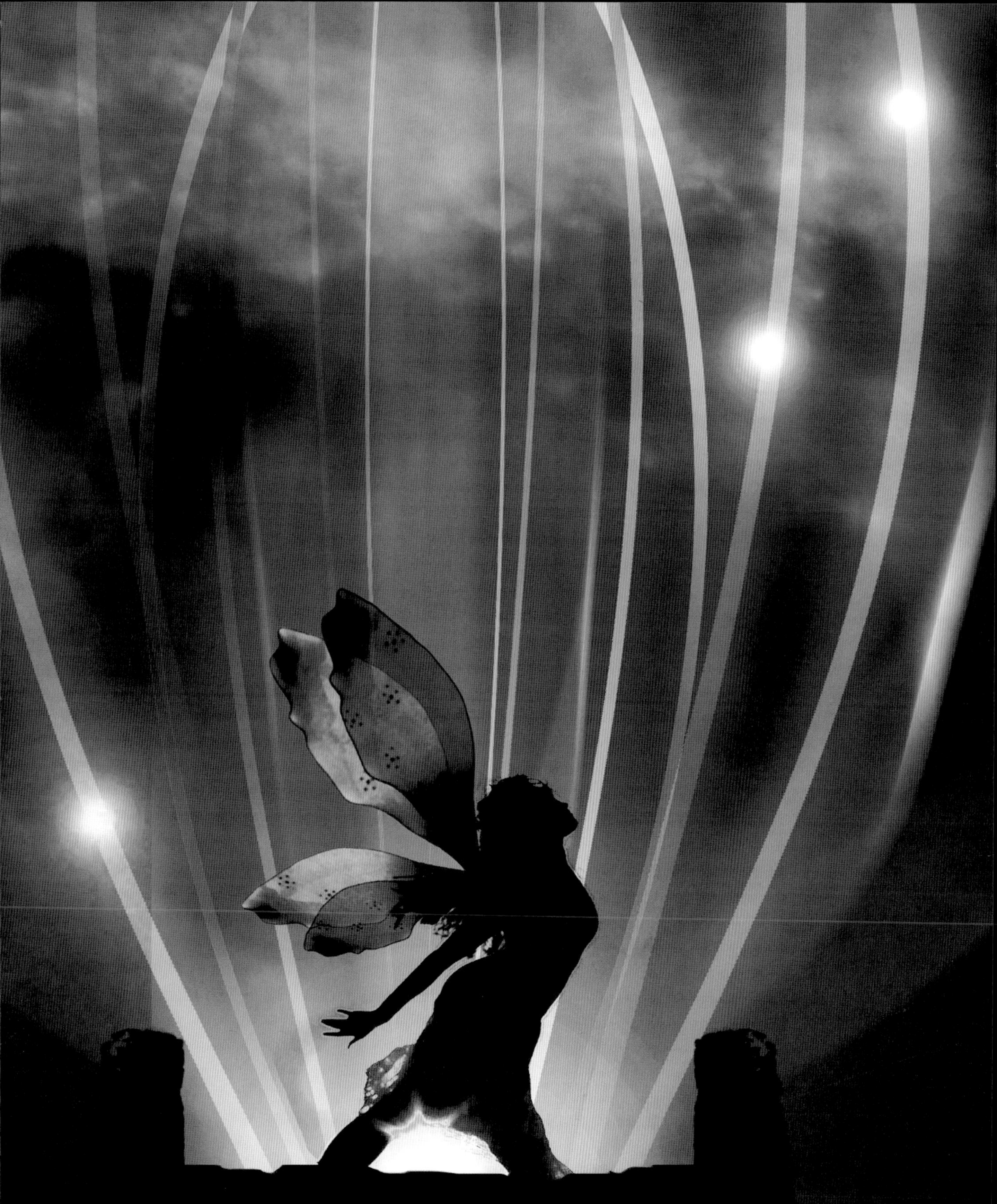

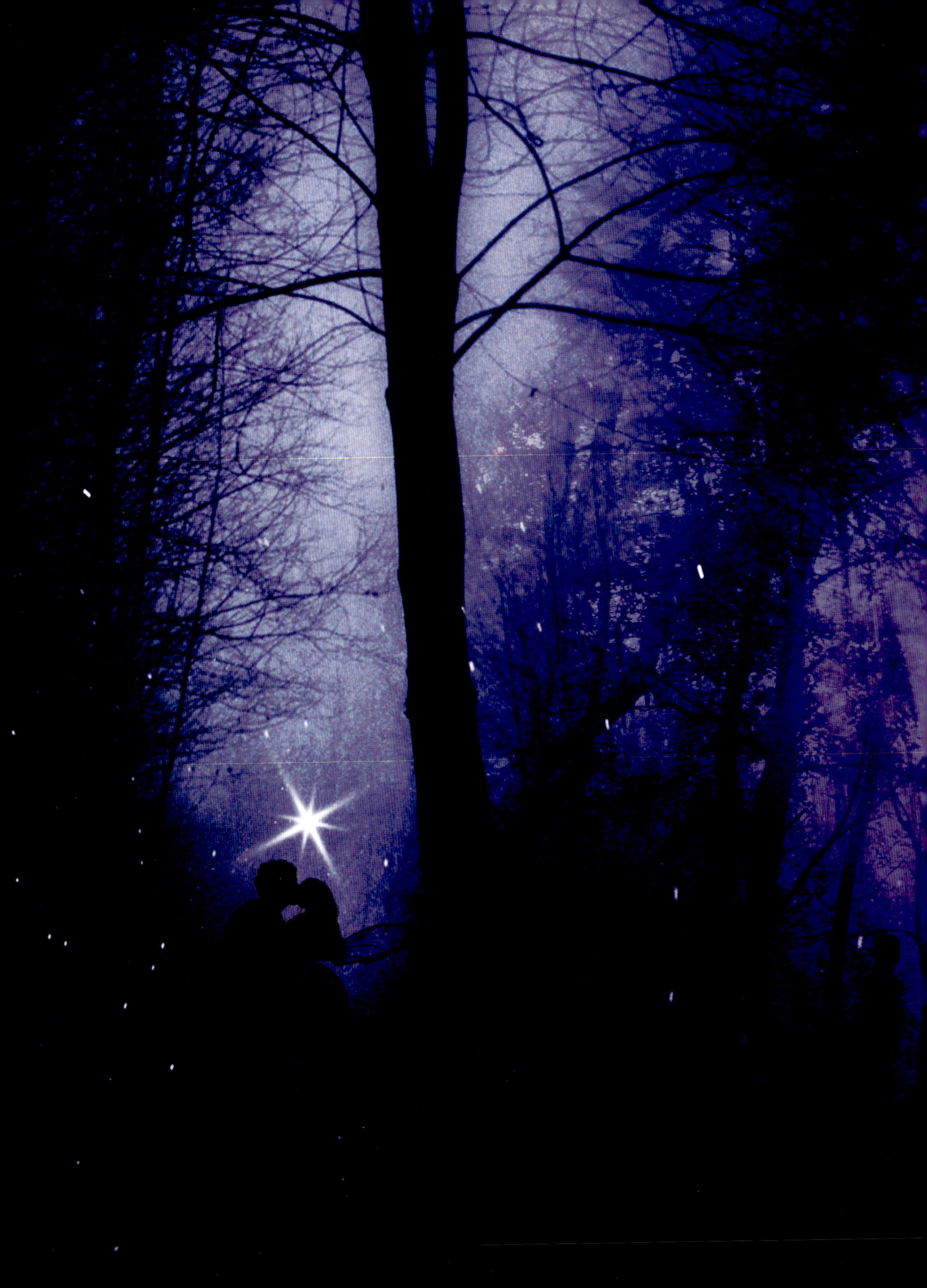

You can still see them, though. In the still moments just before dawn or in the last gleams of the setting sun, you might catch a shard of this bright place bleeding through.

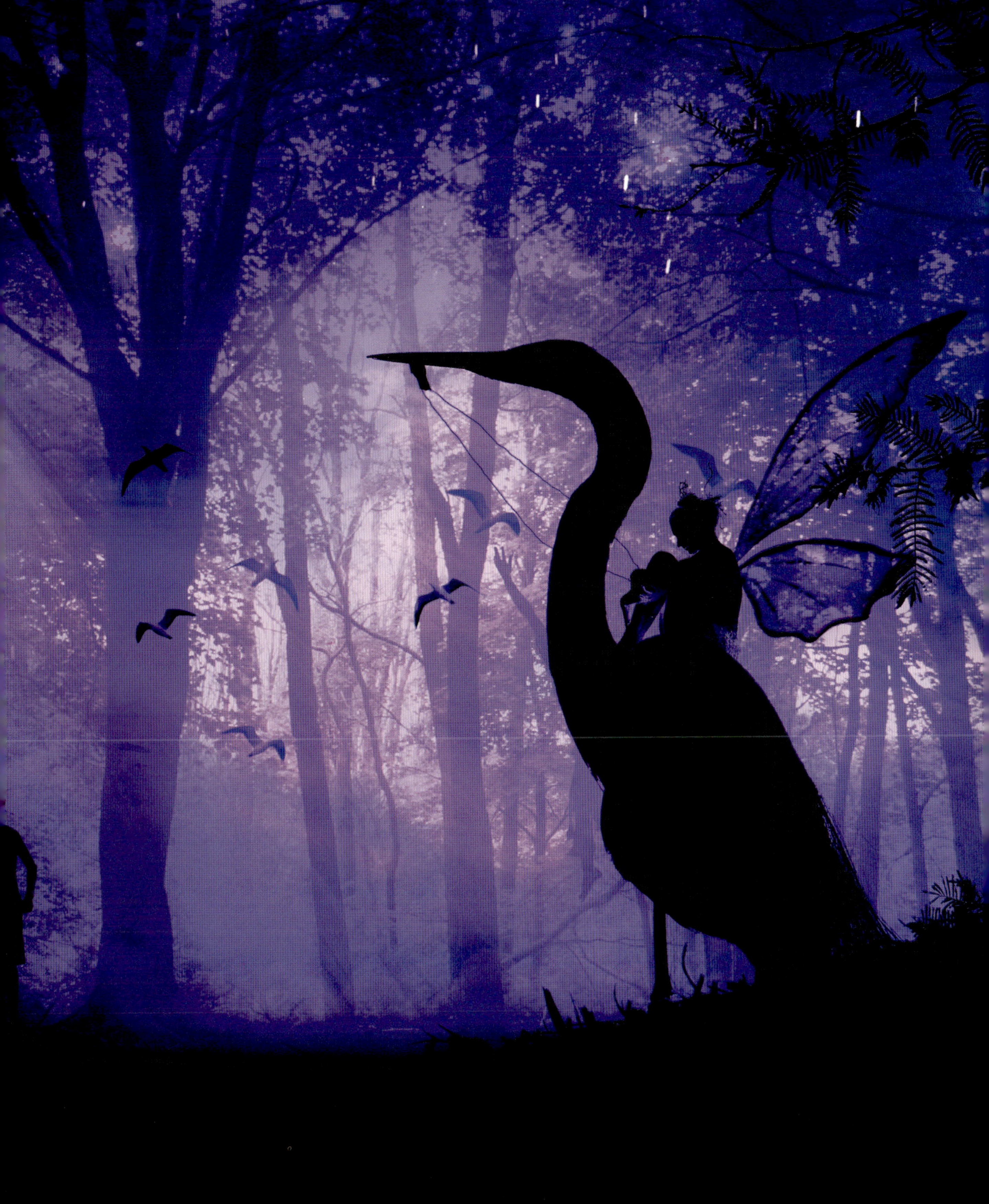

AND IF LUCK SHINES ON YOU, YOU MAY EVEN SEE A QUICK, ILLUSIVE SILHOUETTE, AN ERRANT, FAMILIAR SPARK THAT FADES QUICKLY AS THE LIGHT CHANGES. THOSE WHO HAVE SEEN SUCH A SIGHT HAVE SAID THAT ITS MEMORY LINGERS IN THEIR MIND FOREVER.

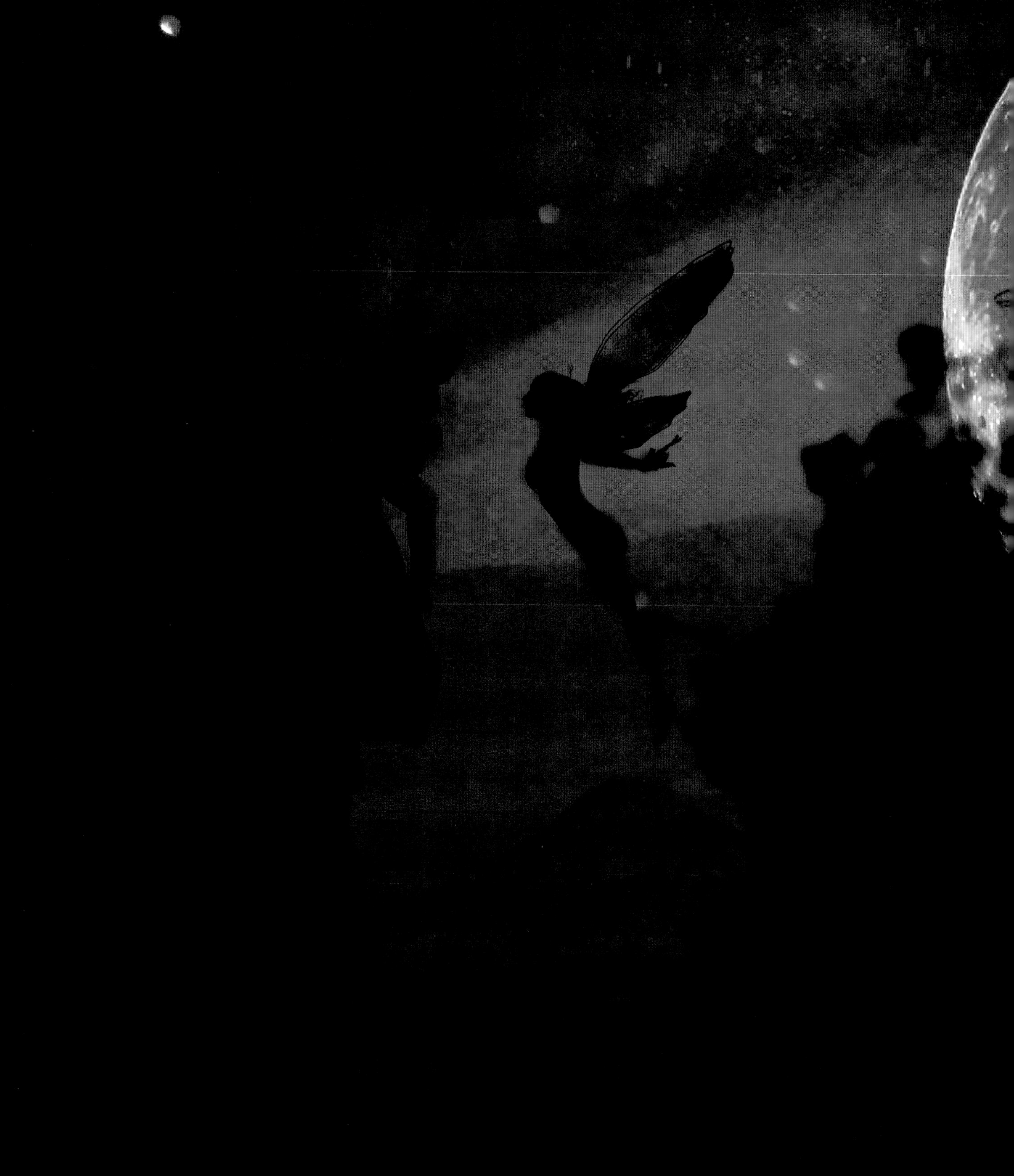

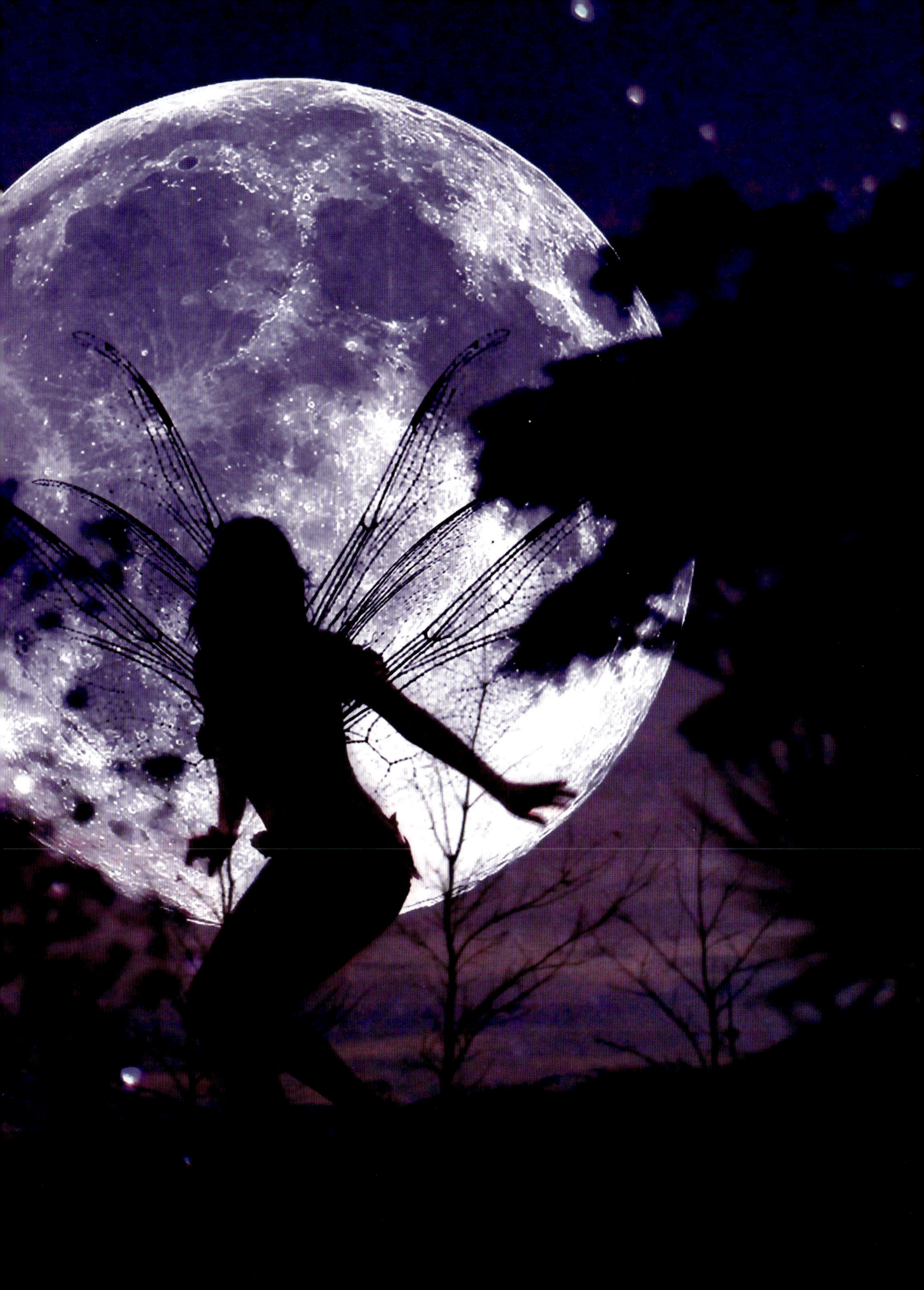

AFTER THE WAR, THE BATTLELANDS WERE BARE AND FALLOW, GIVING UP NO NEW LIFE OR HOPE. IN HER DESPERATION, THE DYING QUEEN CONJURED ONE LAST MAGICK: HER DOOMED ARMY ROSE FROM THE BATTLEGROUND, RE-BORN FROM THE BLOOD SPILLED THERE.

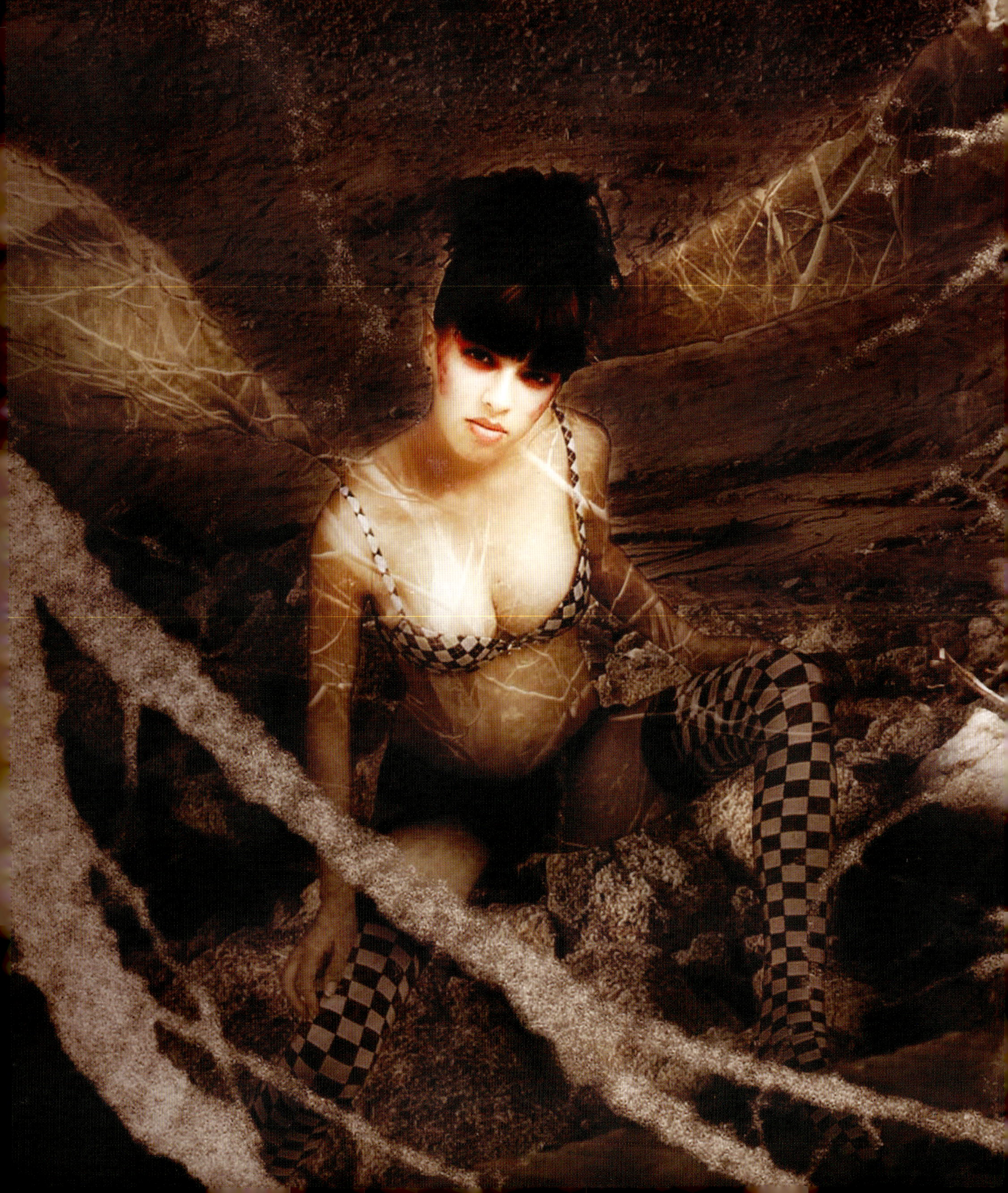

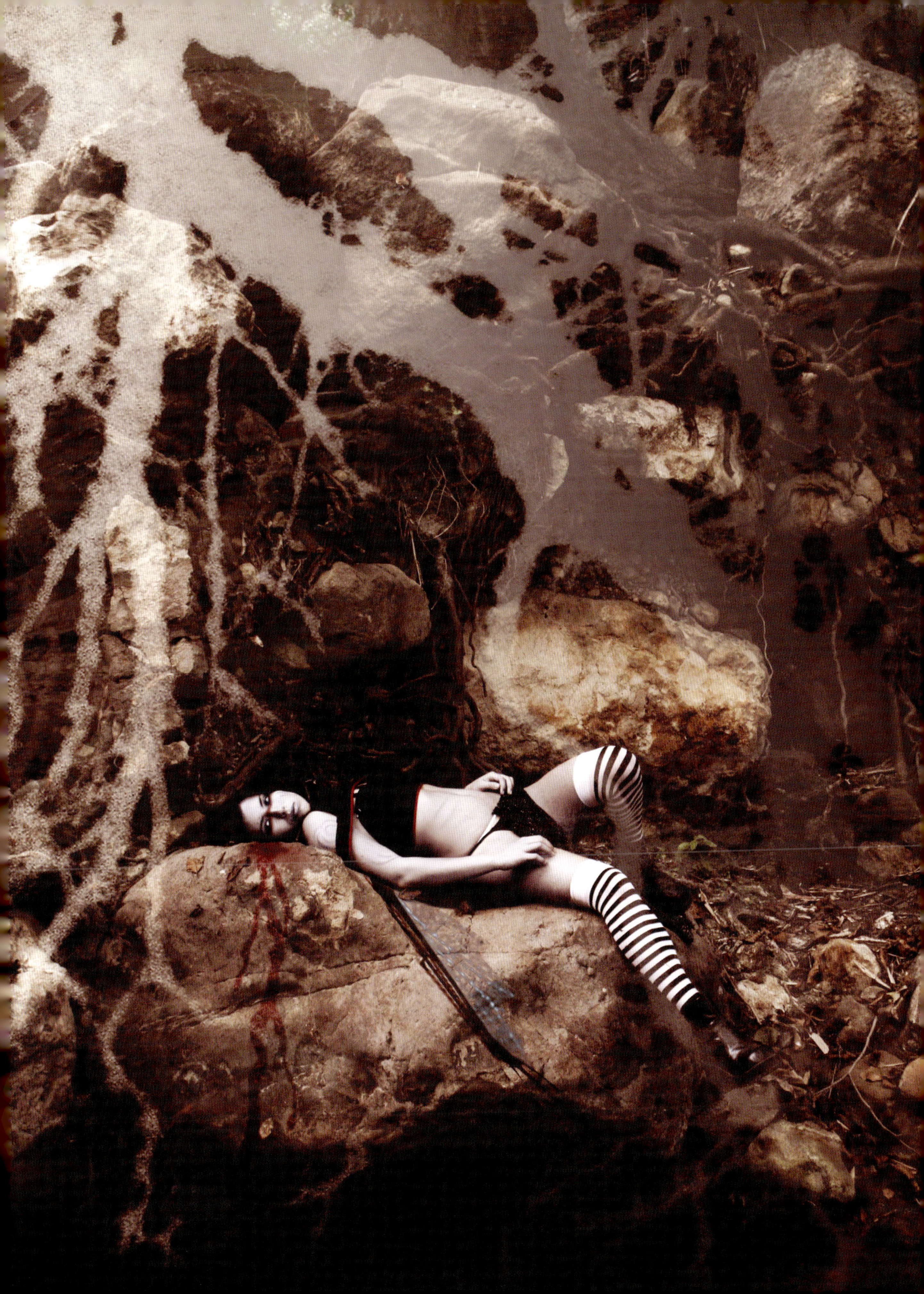

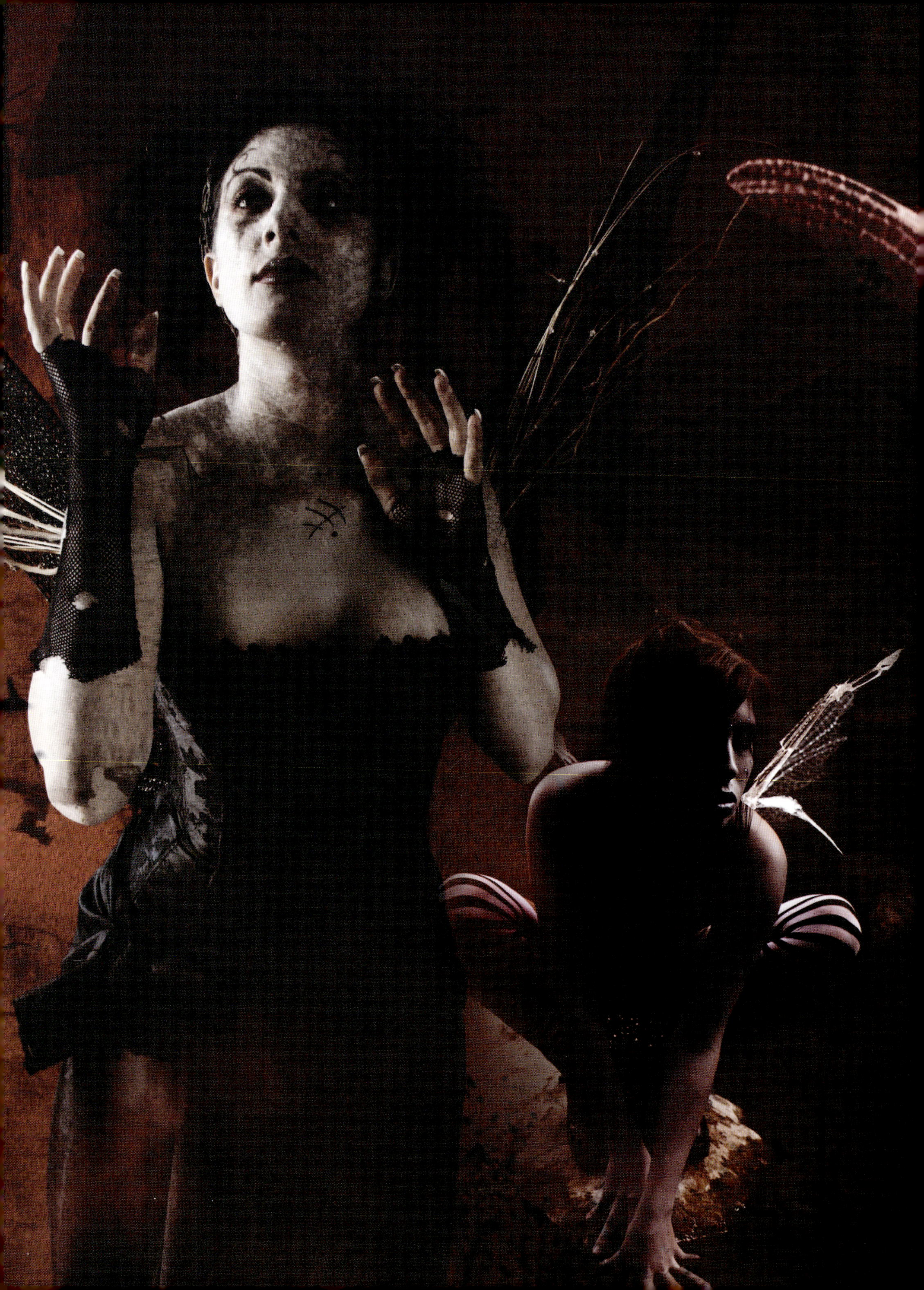

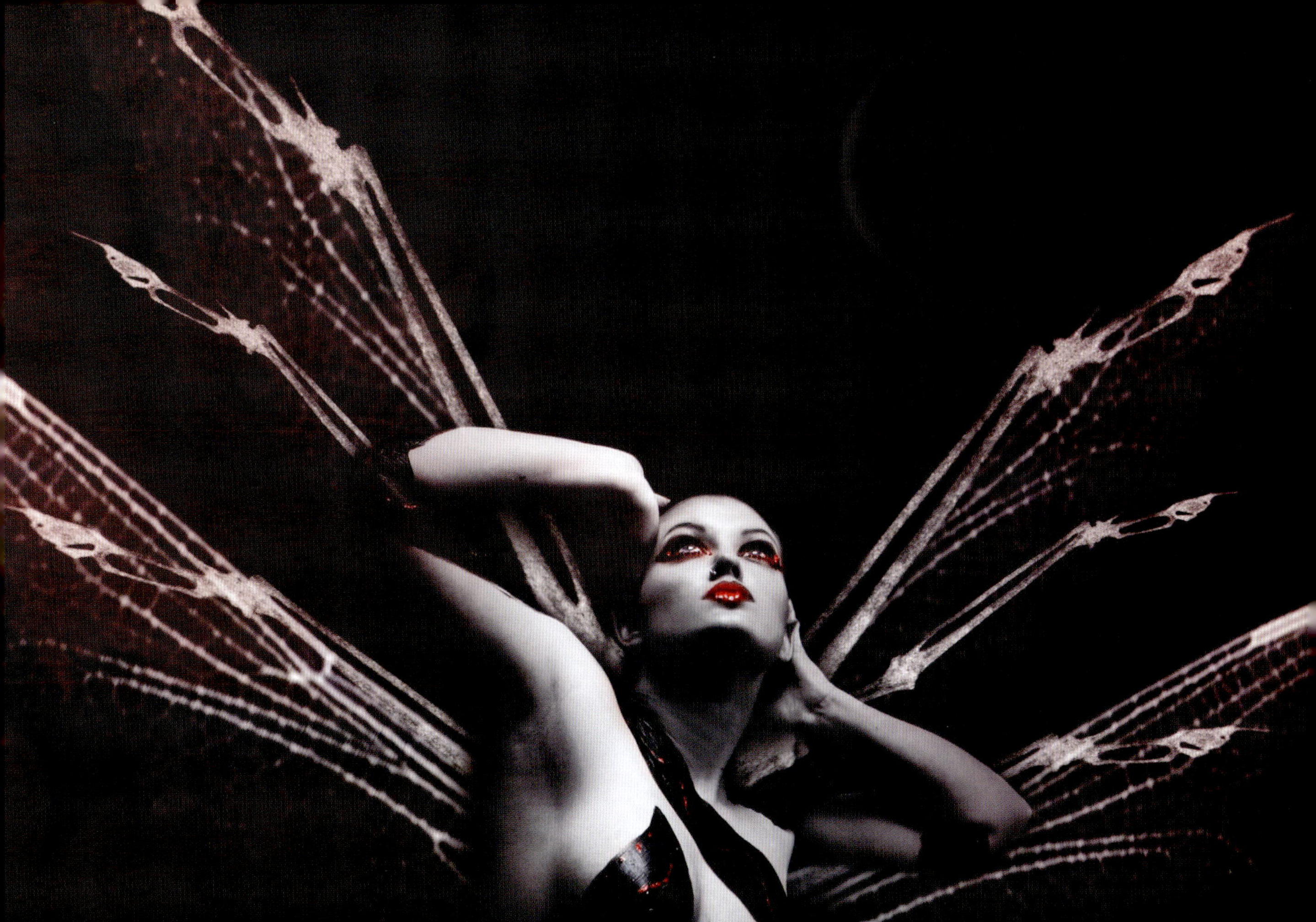

THESE WERE THE DARKLINGS, BORN OF THE BLOOD ELEMENTAL:
COLD, EMPTY, ETERNALLY HUNGRY DESTROYERS OF HOPE, HER ONE LAST
WEAPON AGAINST THE LIGHT, FROZEN IN THE MEMORY OF WAR AND FEAR.

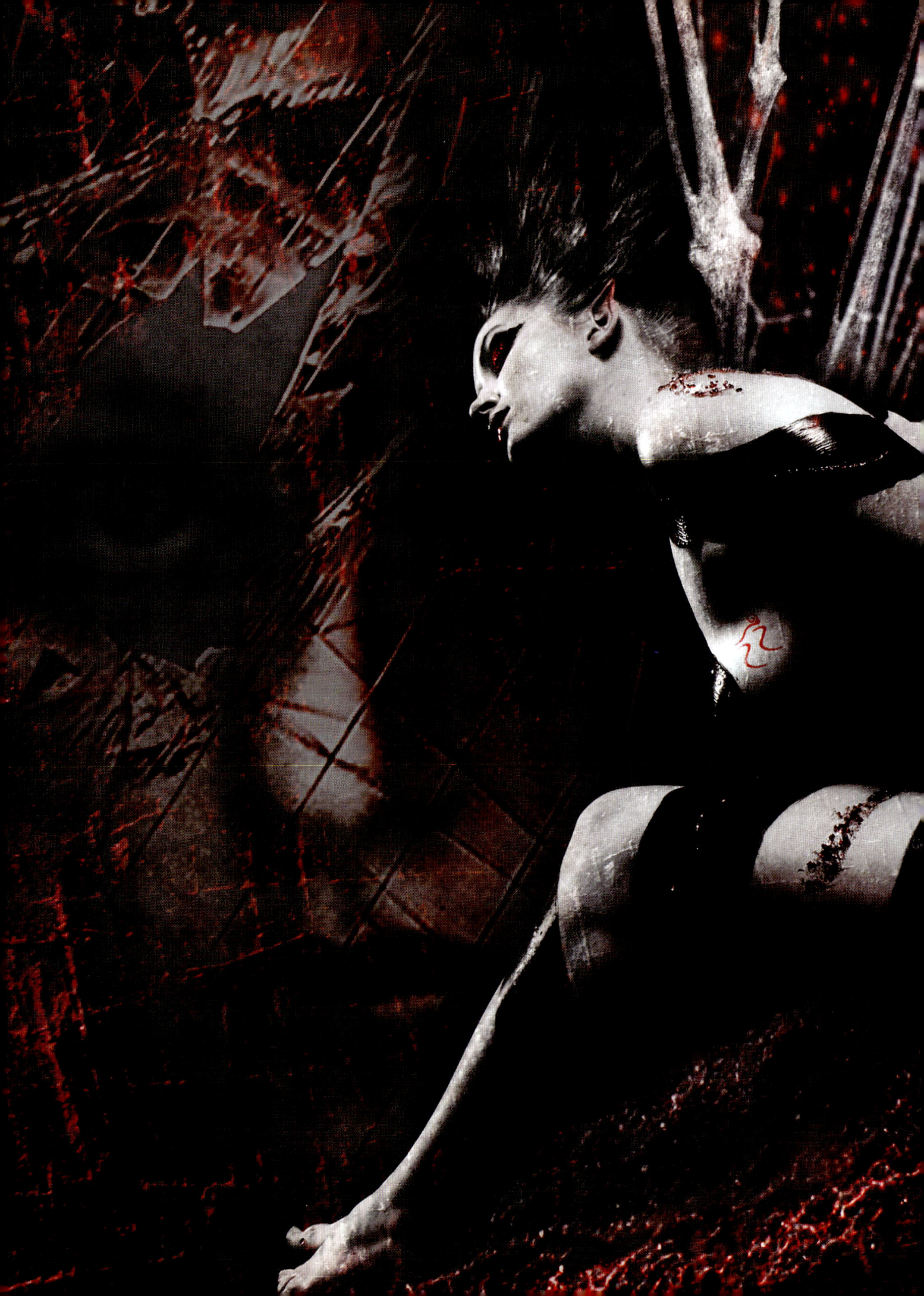

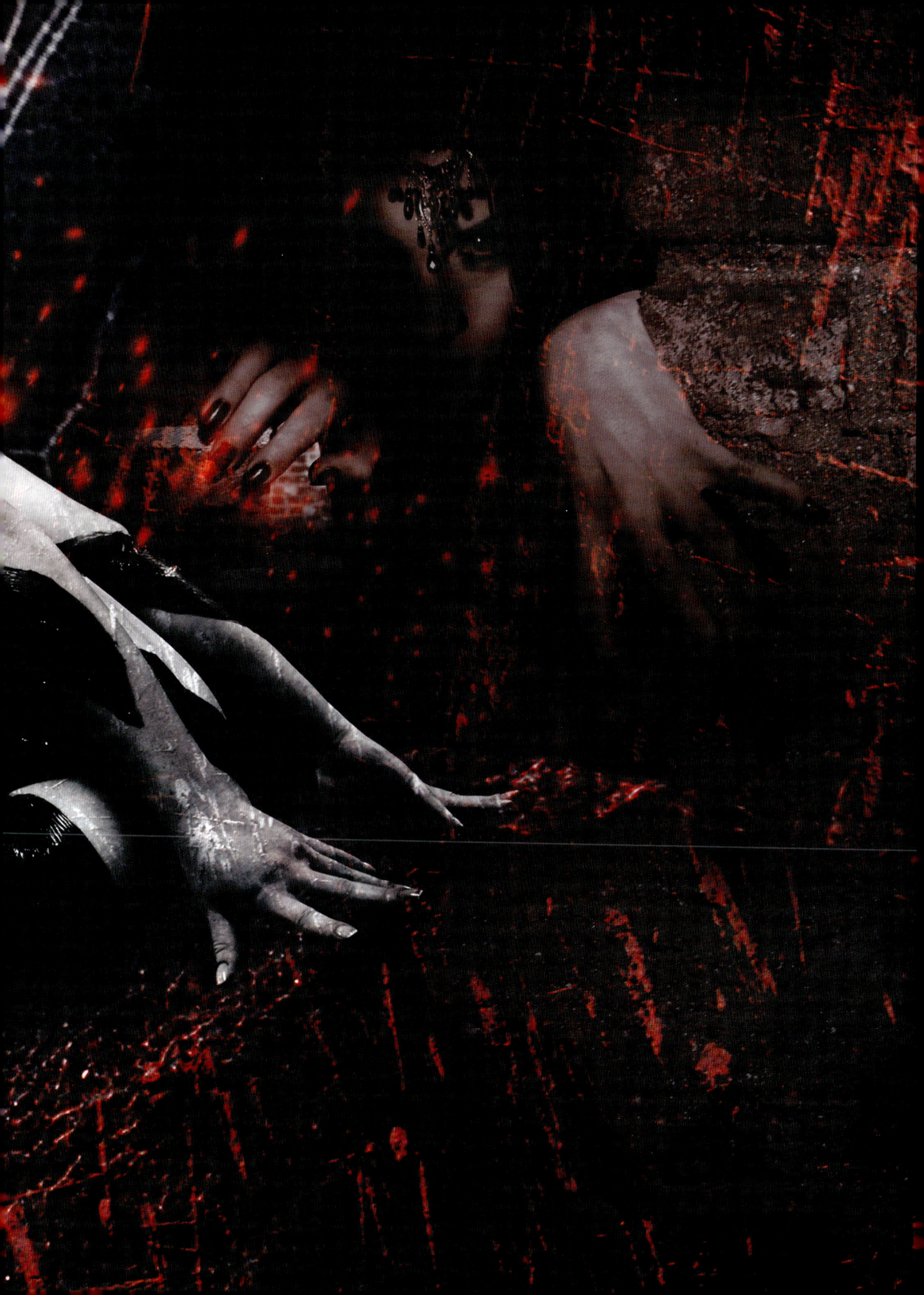

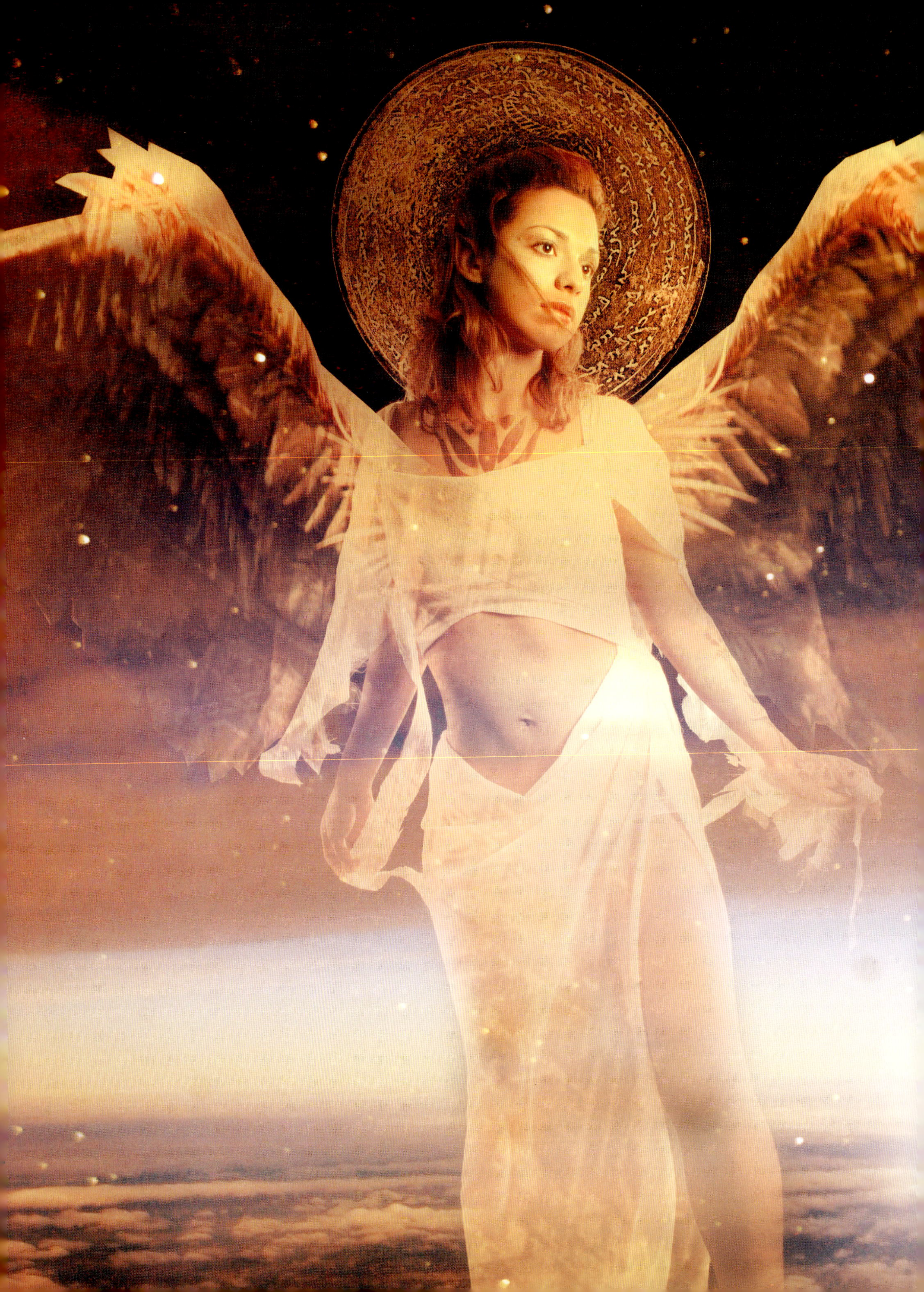

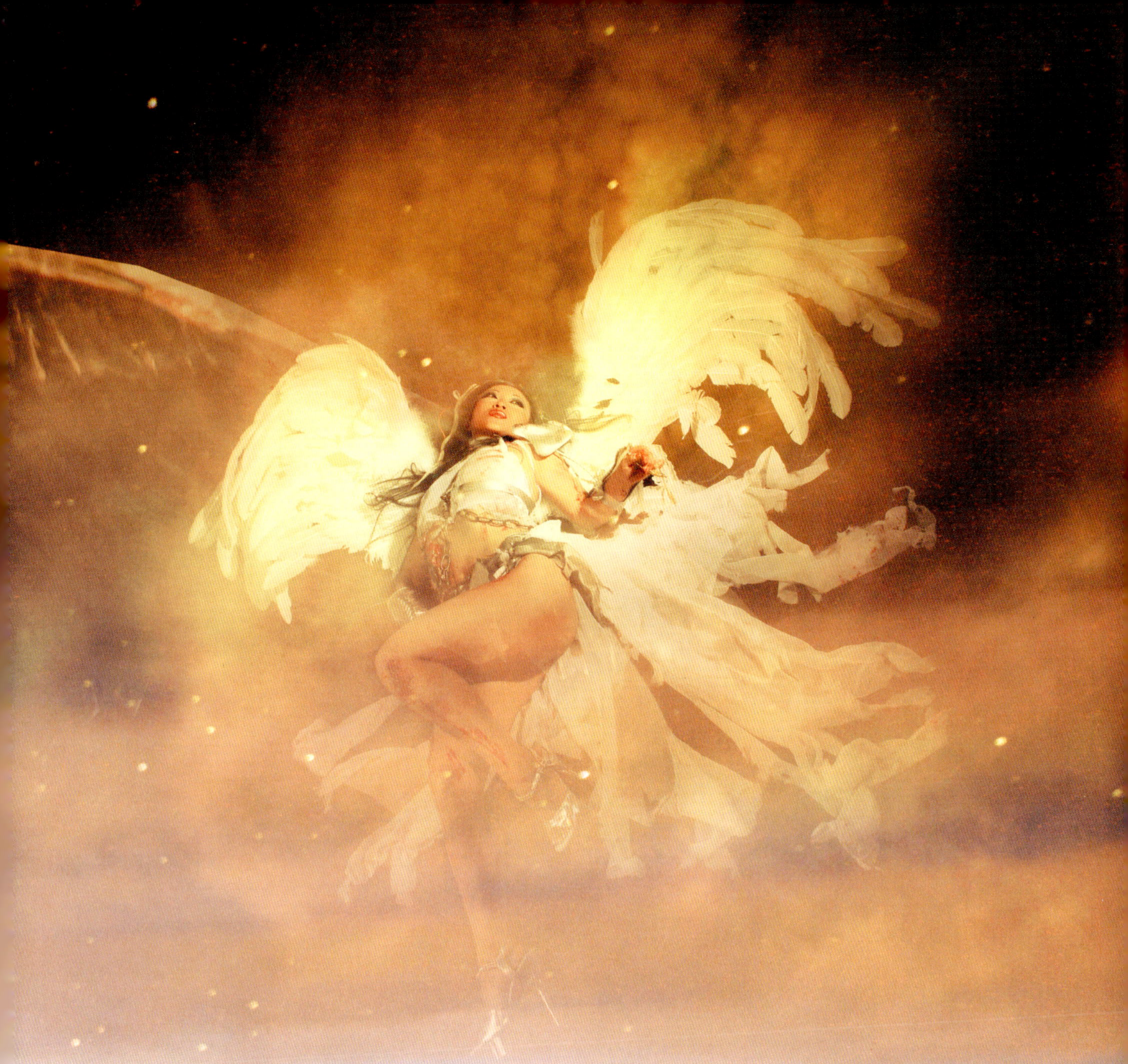

Meanwhile, in Twilight, some faeries grew tired of watching and resolved to use their magic to build a new and better world. They knew they could not do that alone. Cautiously, they moved closer to the world of men, to a world not so far away as Twilight, a place they called E'ven, where they could re-examine the roles between human and magick folk.

In this realm of radiant light, night and darkness held little sway. It was this world that gave birth to the bold and majestic angels of E'ven, divine beings who reveled in their new form and believed that no one on earth would ever wage war upon them again. Their belief was so strong, so passionate, that humans found themselves more and more affected by their angelic light and slowly opened their hearts to the elemental spirits they had feared for so long.

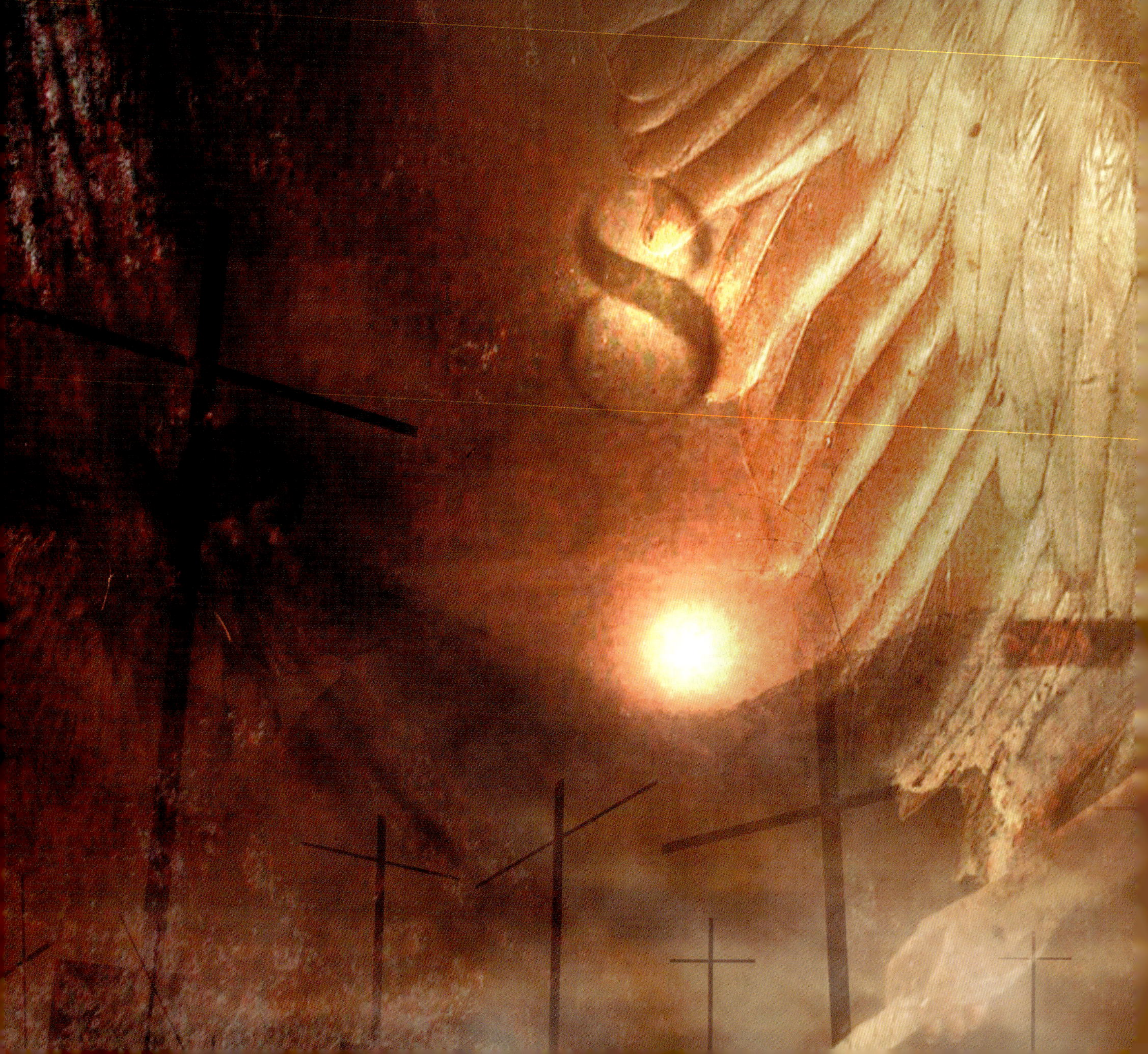

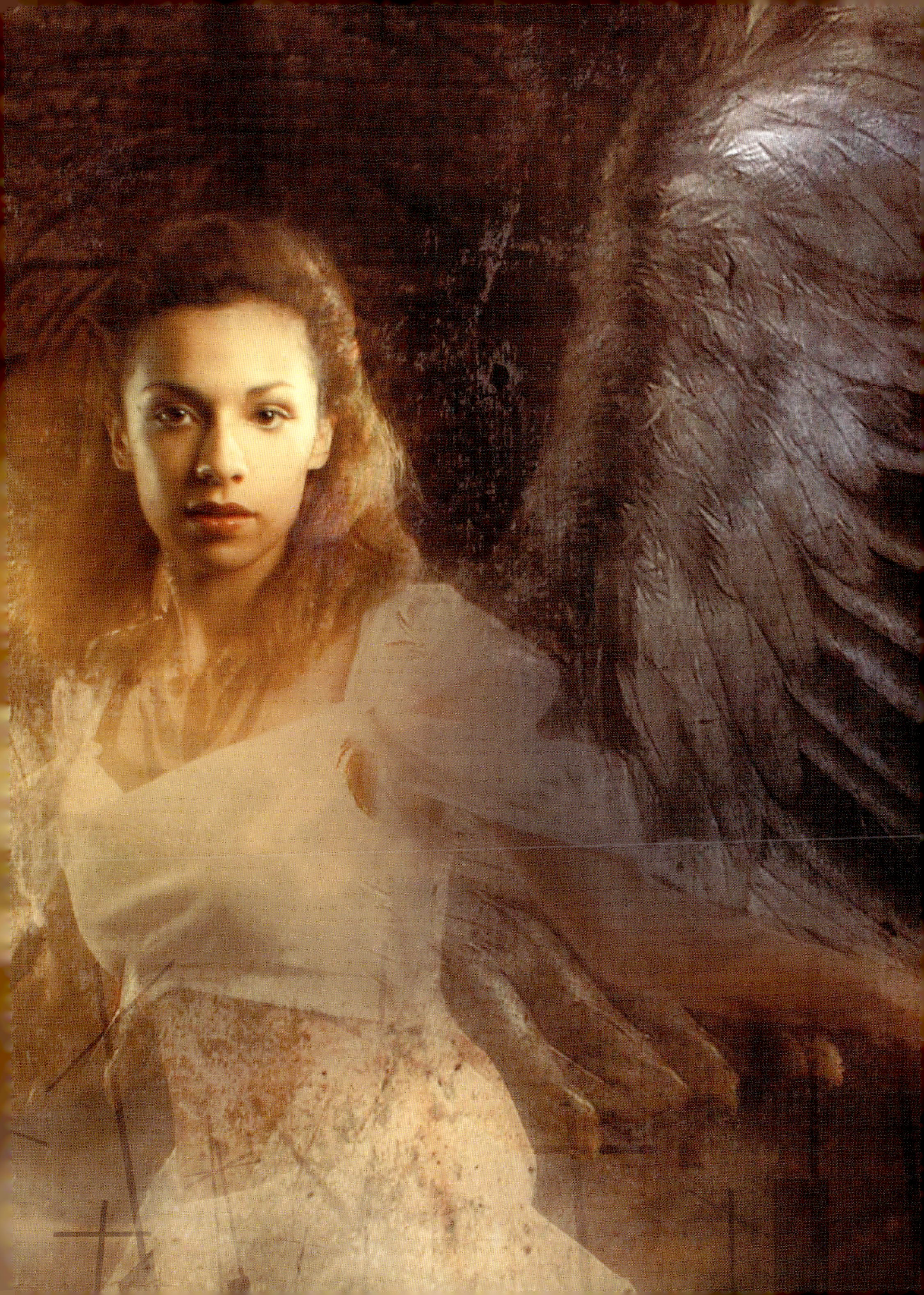

THE OLD HISTORY FADED INTO MYTH, AND A NEW HISTORY OF DIVINE ANGELIC LIGHT WAS BORN TO HELP HEAL THE ANCIENT WOUND OF THESE WORLDS. WITH THIS NEW DIVINE PLAN ANGELS WOULD RULE WITH LIGHT ON A BLIND PEOPLE, AND TWO THOUSAND YEARS WOULD PASS BEFORE ANOTHER FAERIE WOULD STEP FOOT INTO THE WORLD OF MEN.

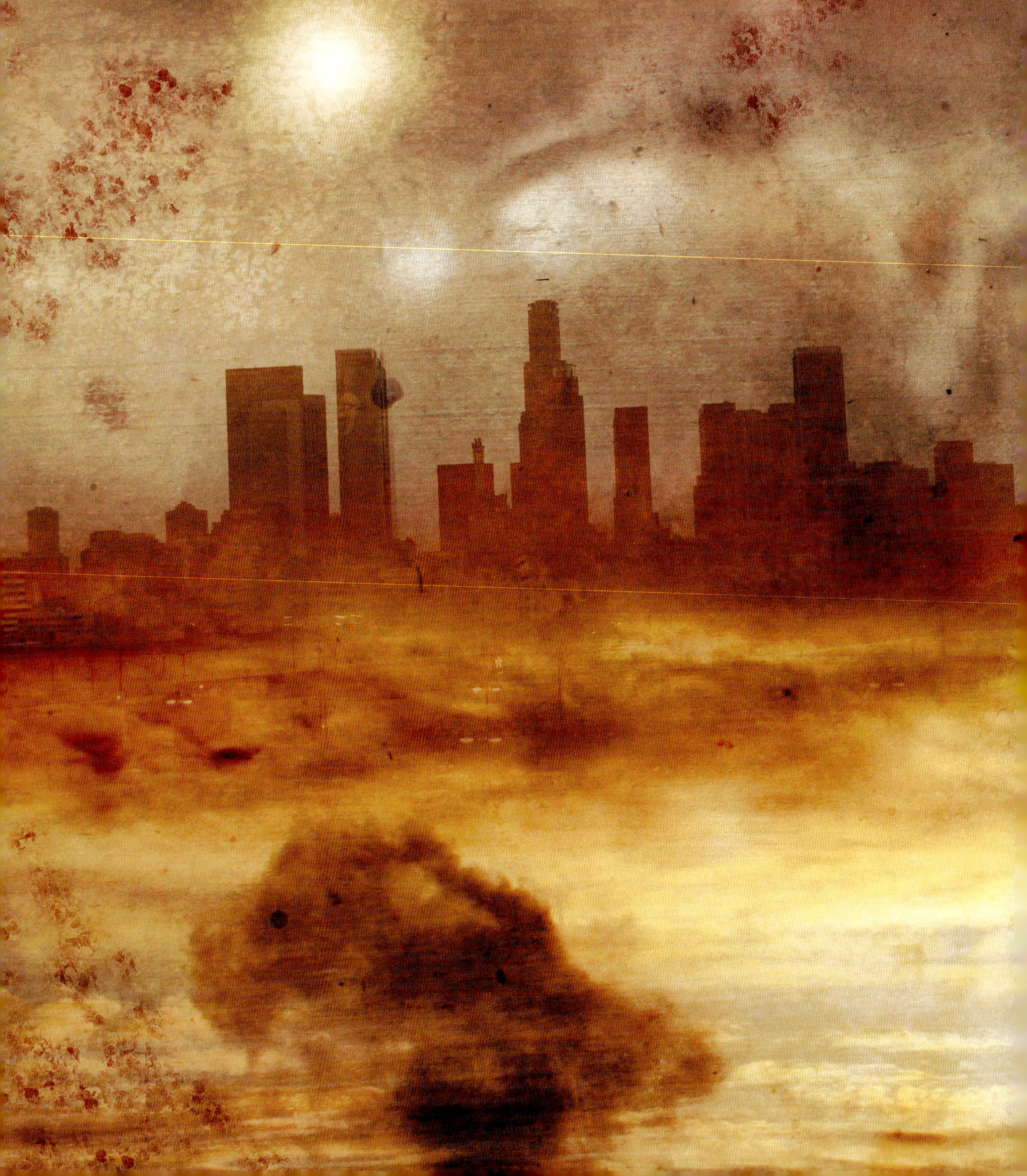

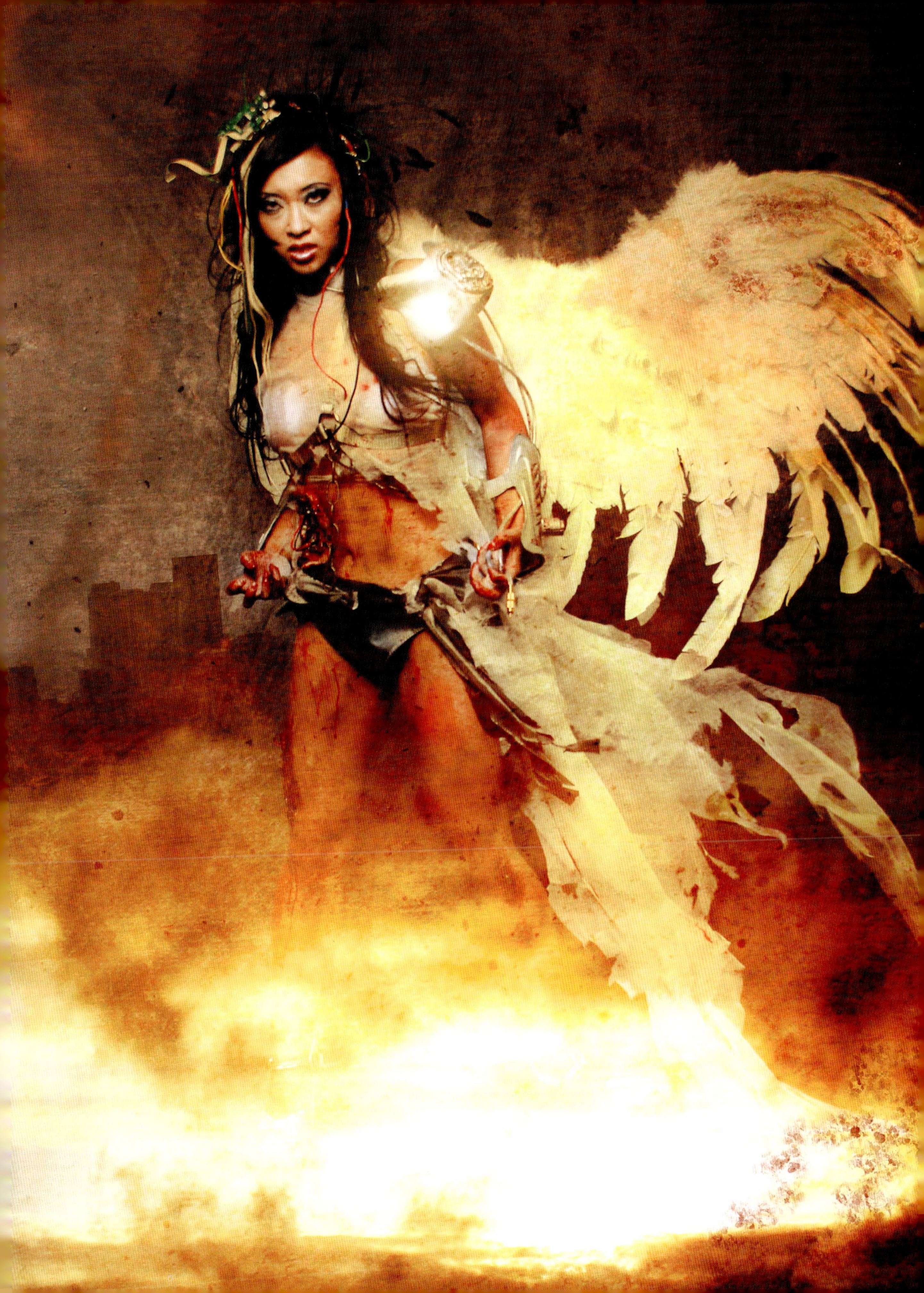

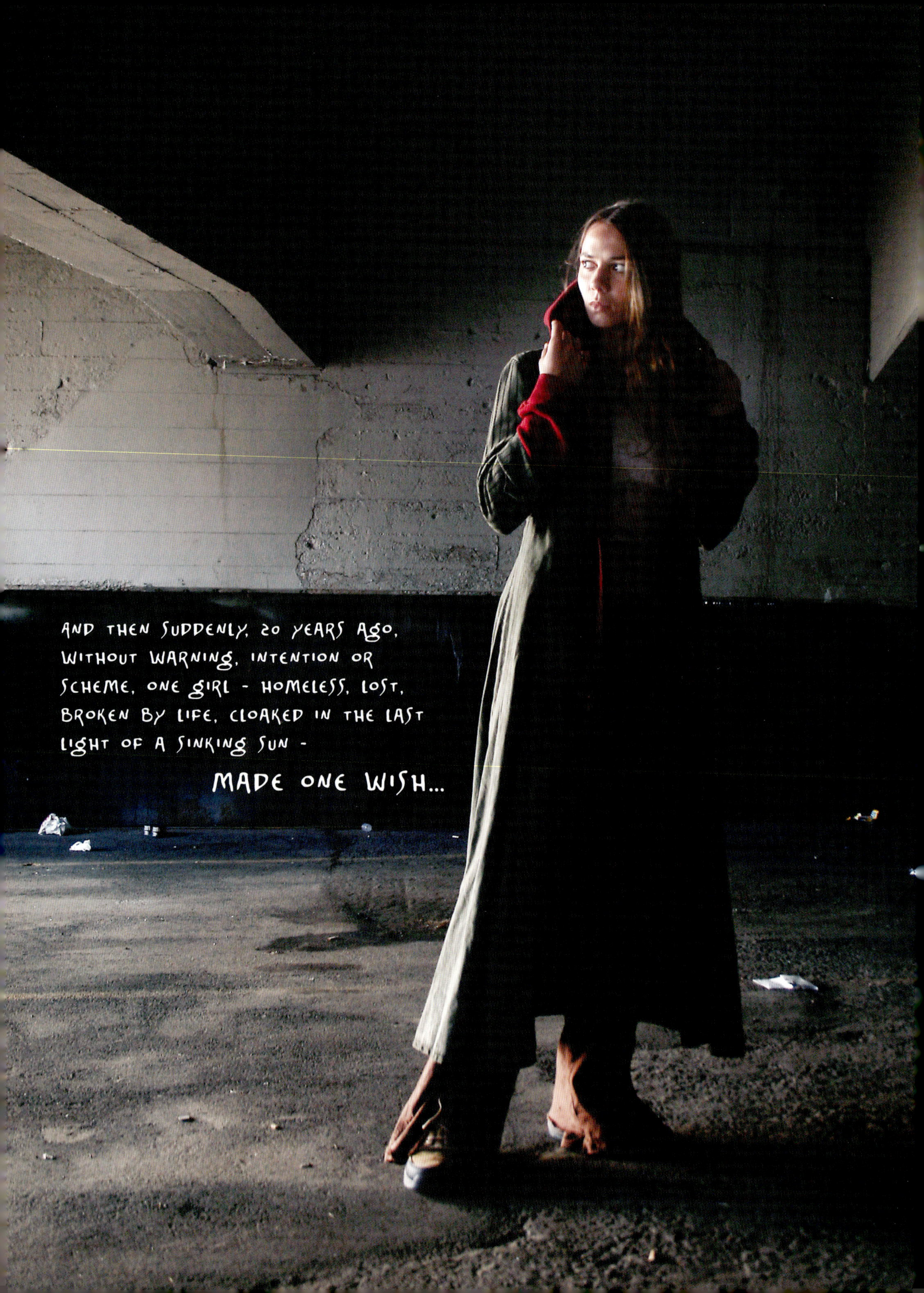

And then suddenly, 20 years ago, without warning, intention or scheme, one girl - homeless, lost, broken by life, cloaked in the last light of a sinking sun -

MADE ONE WISH...

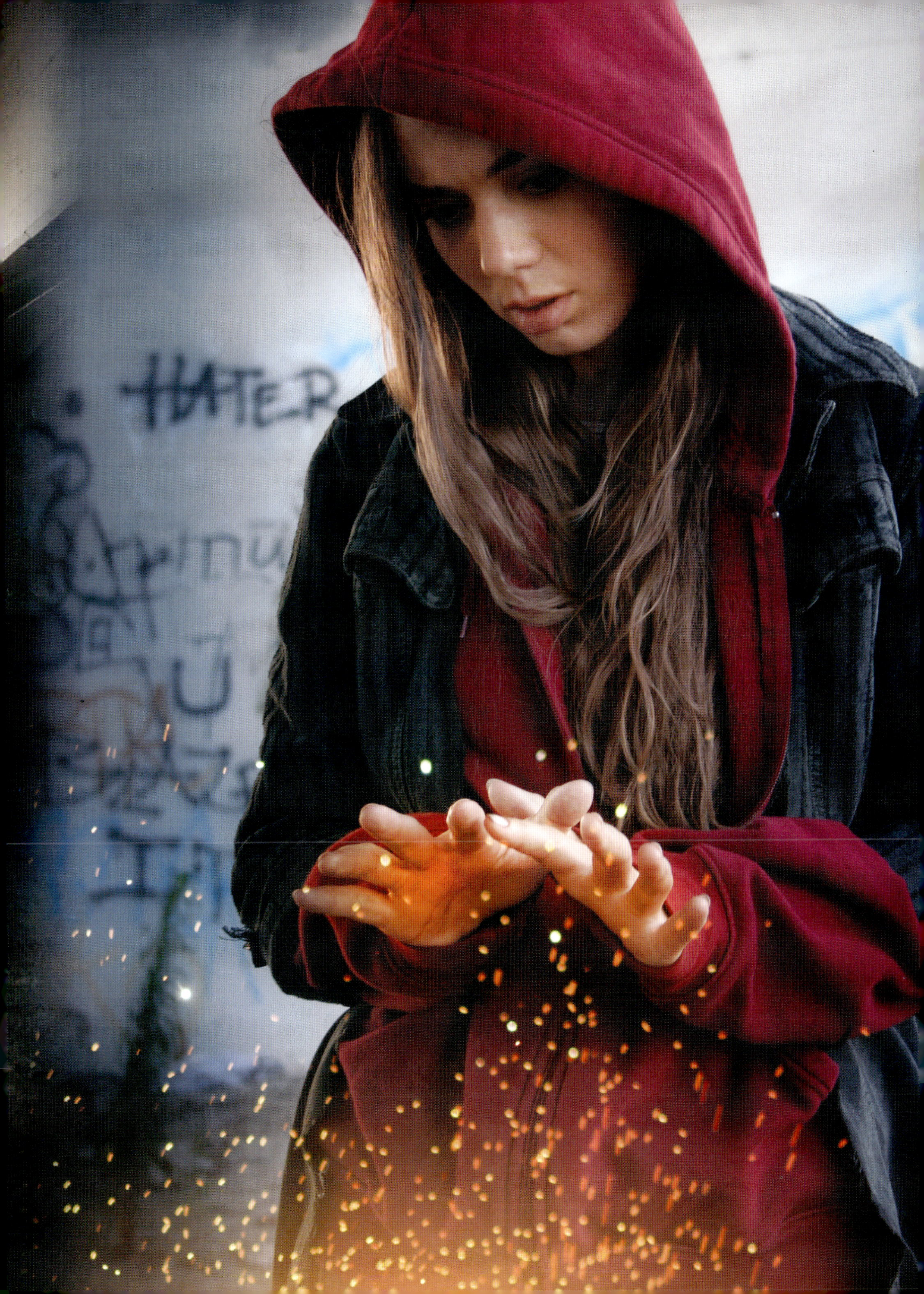
HATER

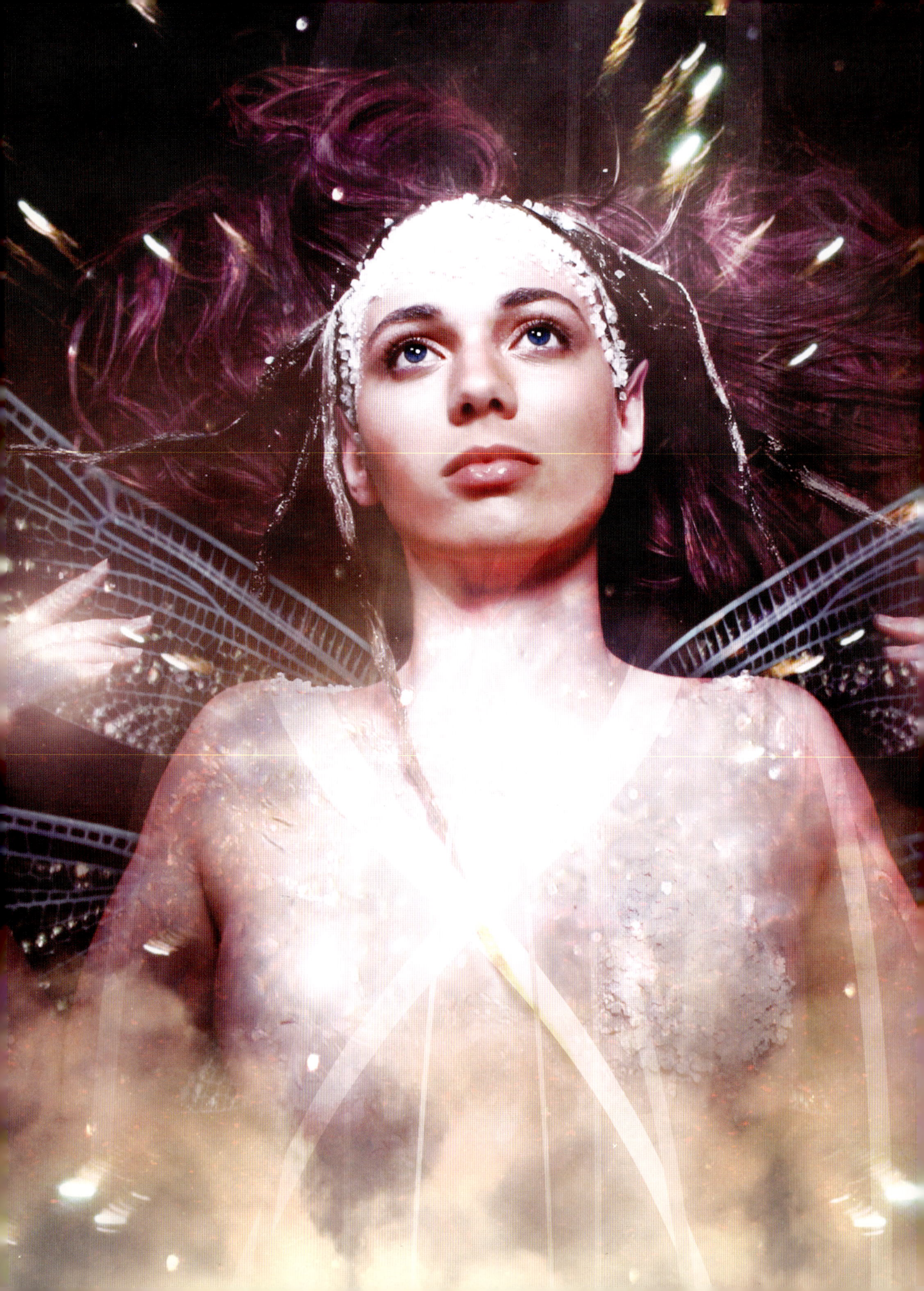

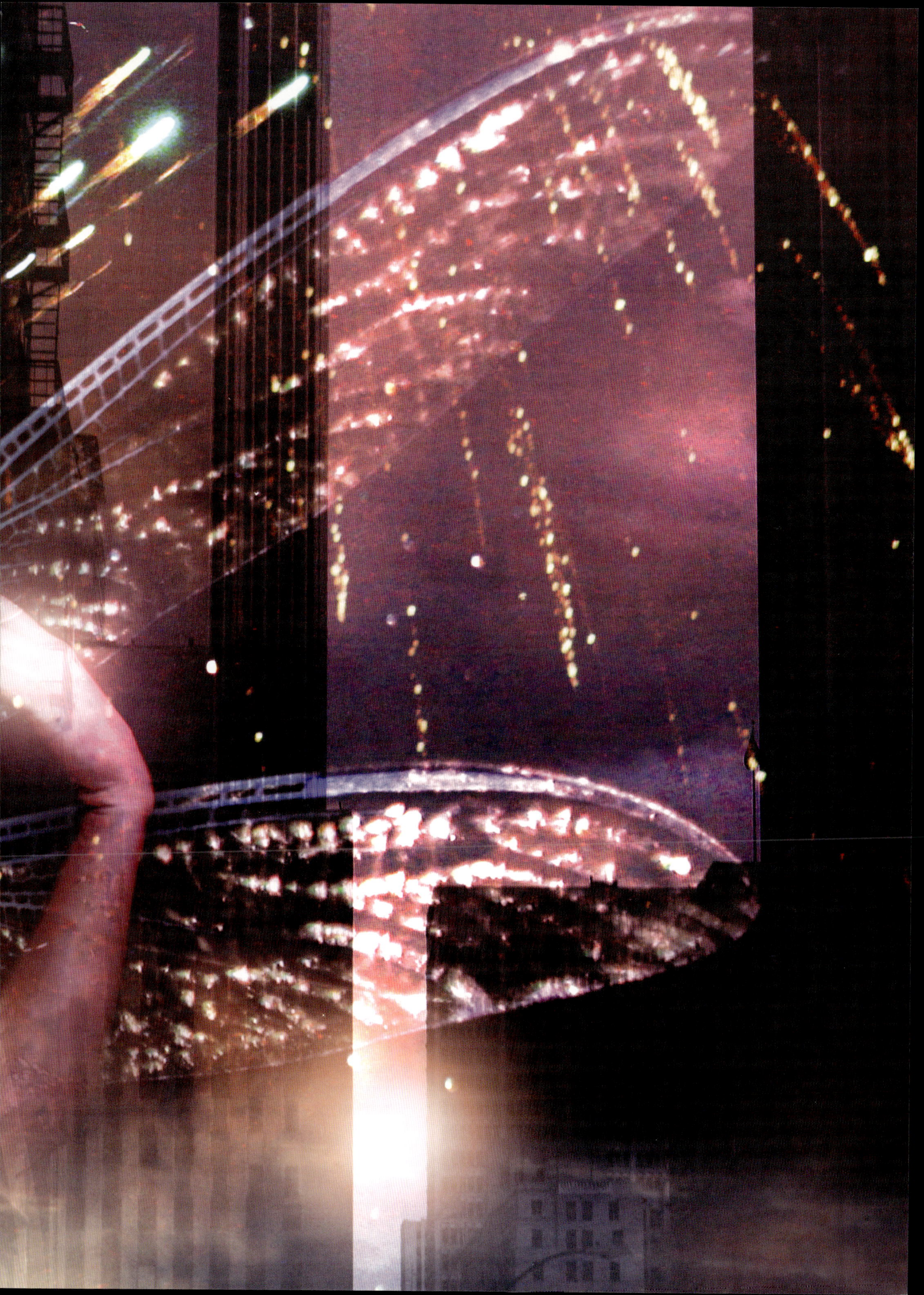

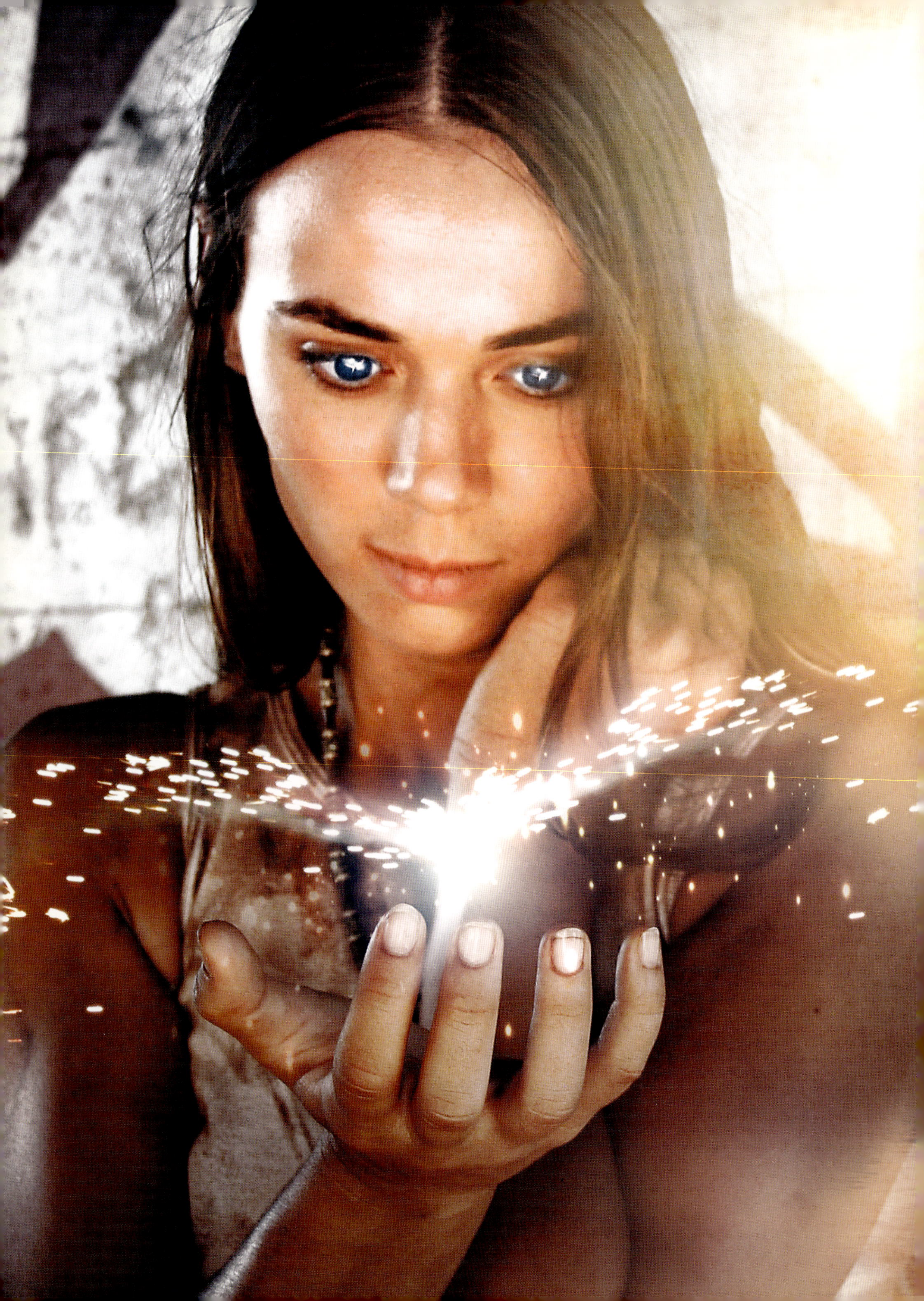

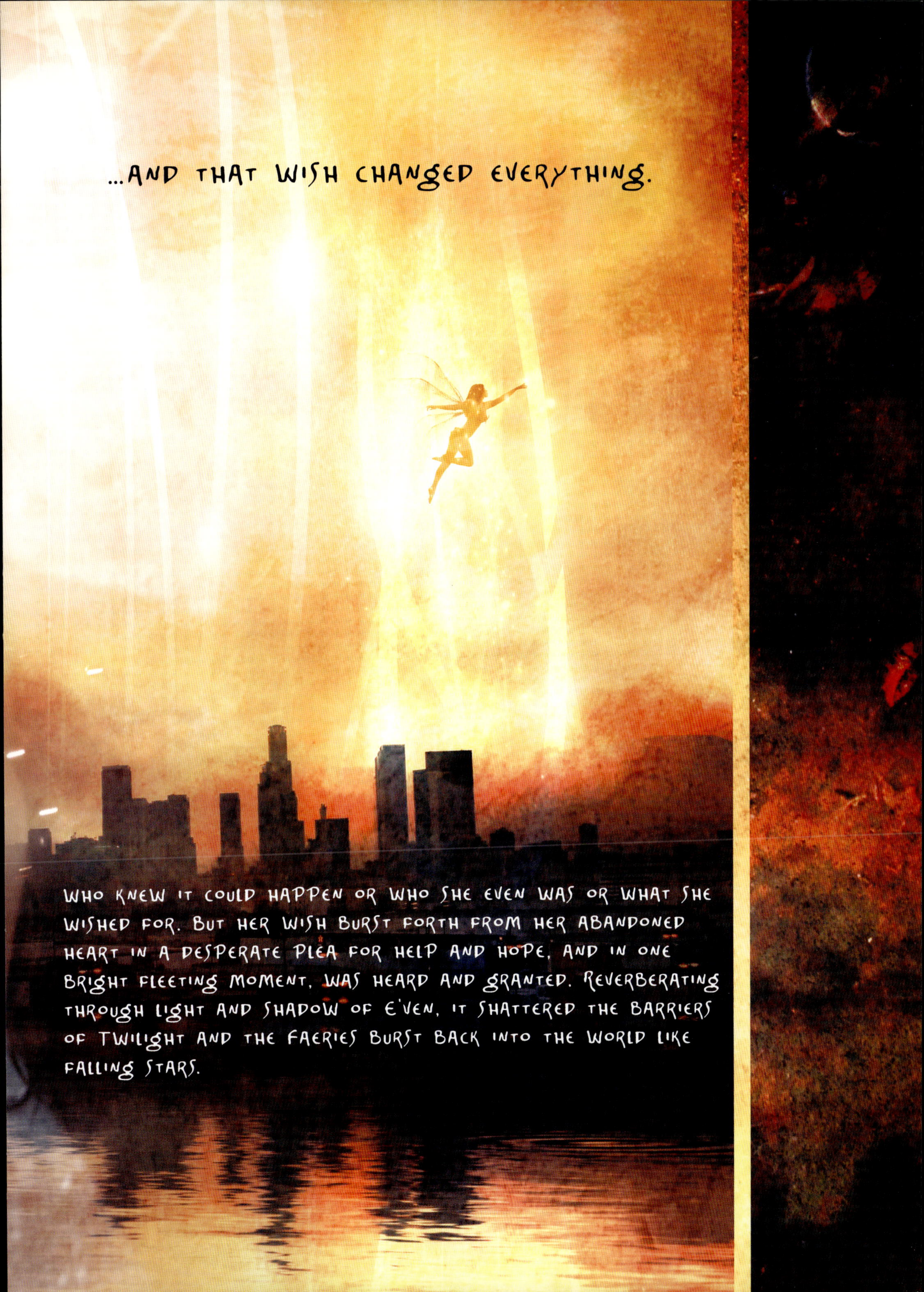
...AND THAT WISH CHANGED EVERYTHING.
WHO KNEW IT COULD HAPPEN OR WHO SHE EVEN WAS OR WHAT SHE WISHED FOR. BUT HER WISH BURST FORTH FROM HER ABANDONED HEART IN A DESPERATE PLEA FOR HELP AND HOPE, AND IN ONE BRIGHT FLEETING MOMENT, WAS HEARD AND GRANTED. REVERBERATING THROUGH LIGHT AND SHADOW OF E'VEN, IT SHATTERED THE BARRIERS OF TWILIGHT AND THE FAERIES BURST BACK INTO THE WORLD LIKE FALLING STARS.

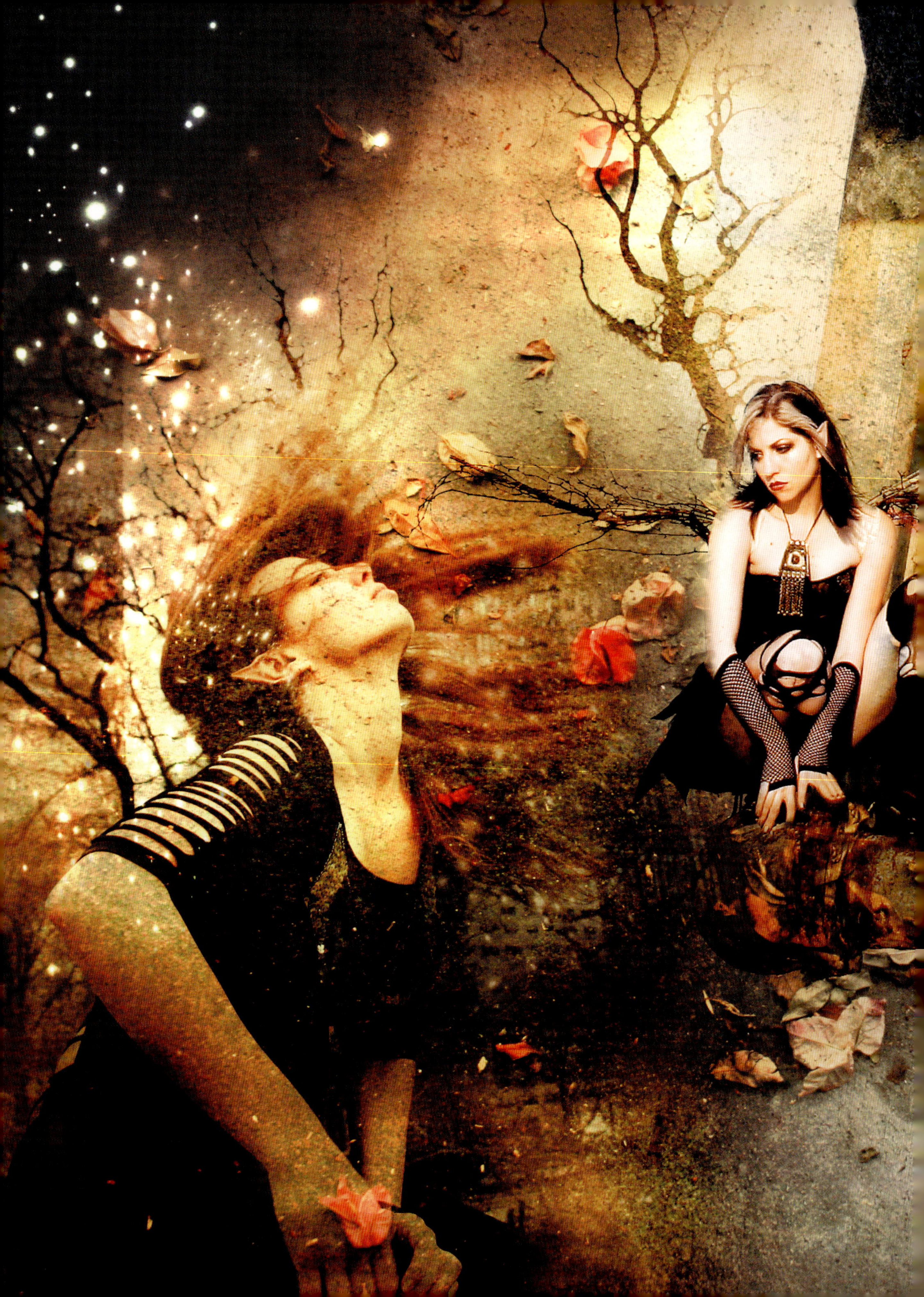

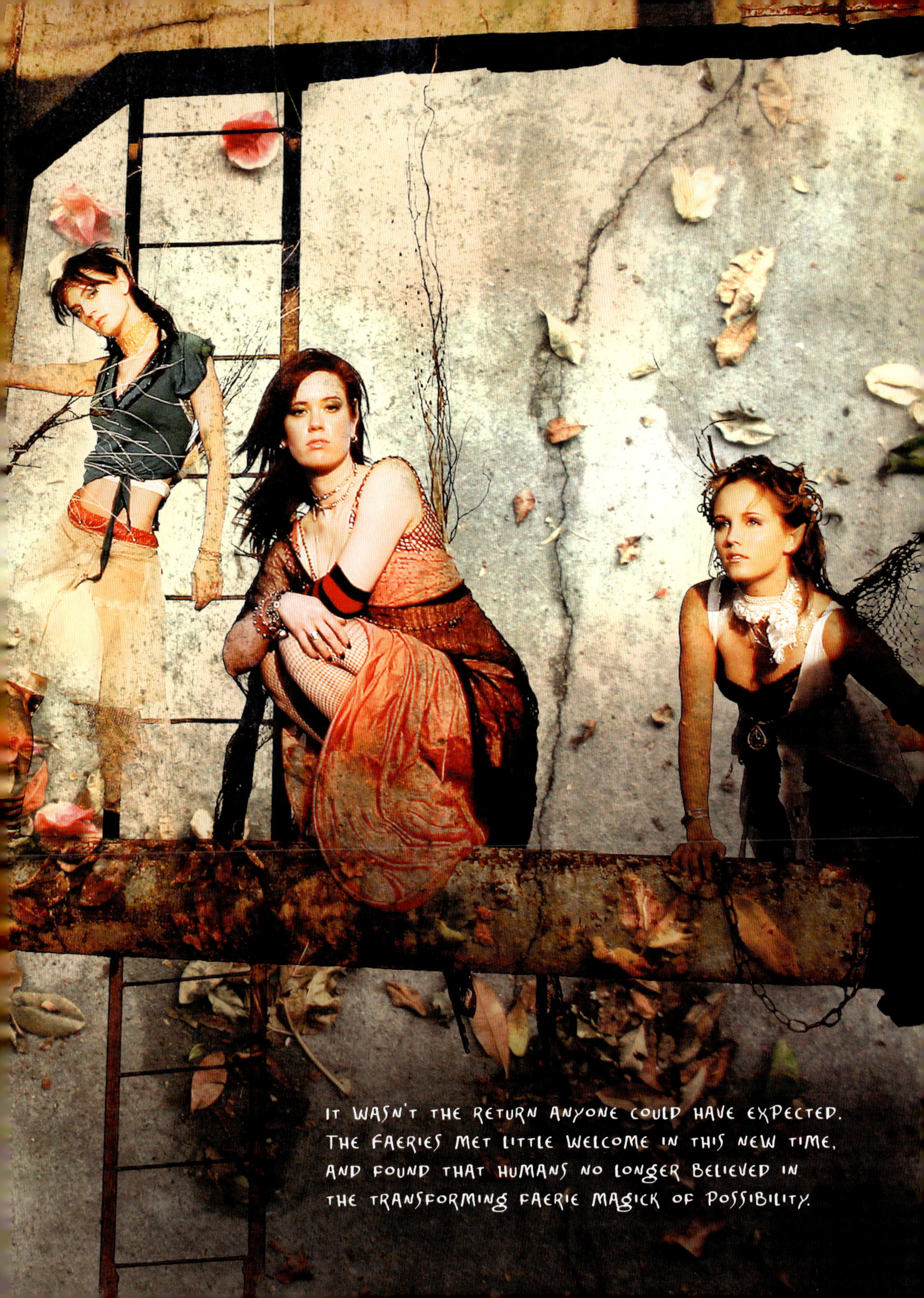

IT WASN'T THE RETURN ANYONE COULD HAVE EXPECTED. THE FAERIES MET LITTLE WELCOME IN THIS NEW TIME, AND FOUND THAT HUMANS NO LONGER BELIEVED IN THE TRANSFORMING FAERIE MAGICK OF POSSIBILITY.

THEY ALSO FOUND THE LAND MUCH CHANGED, SCARRED BY MISUSE AND "PROGRESS." AWASH IN DISAPPOINTMENT, SOME OF THEM SANK DEEP INTO DARKNESS.

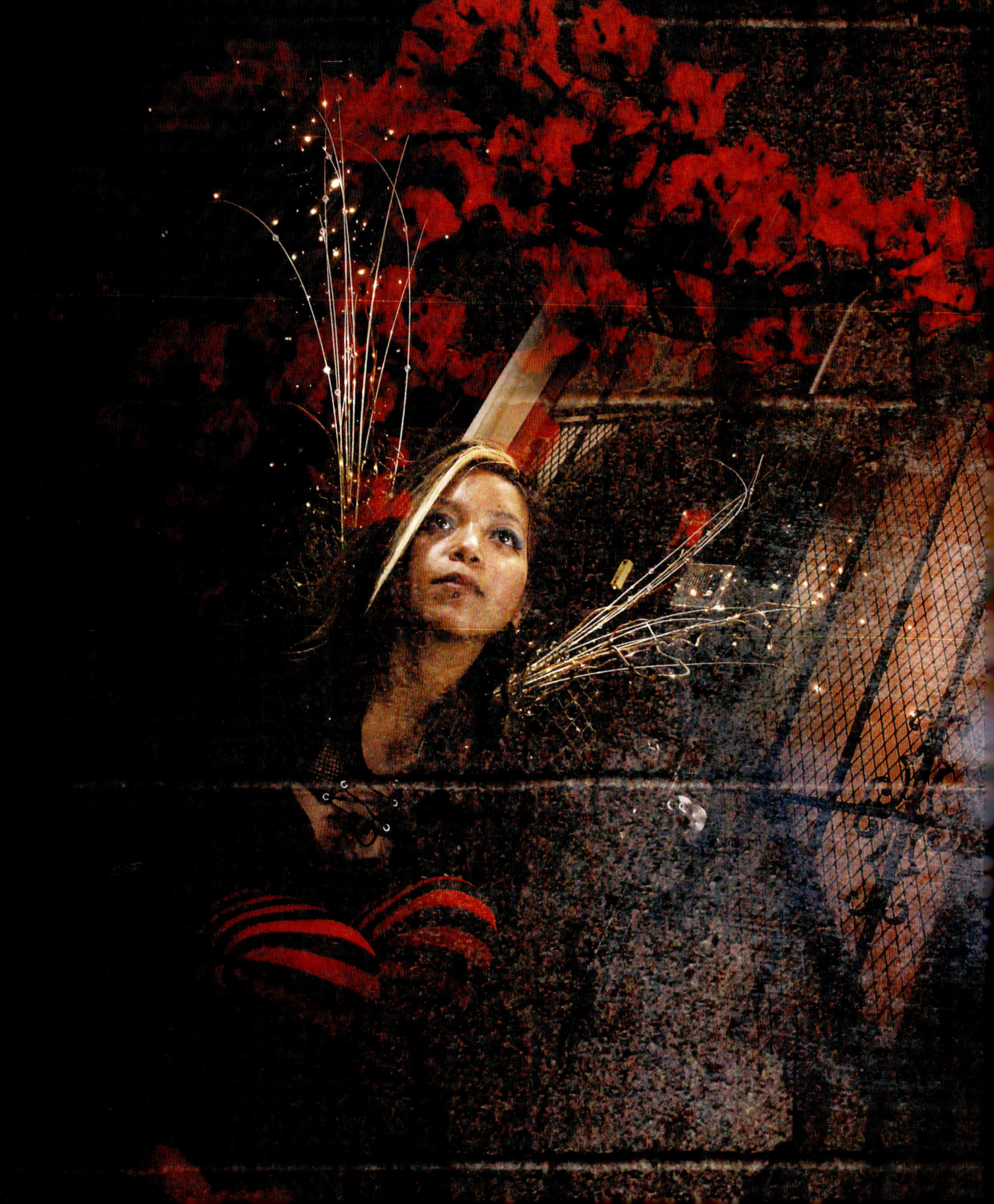

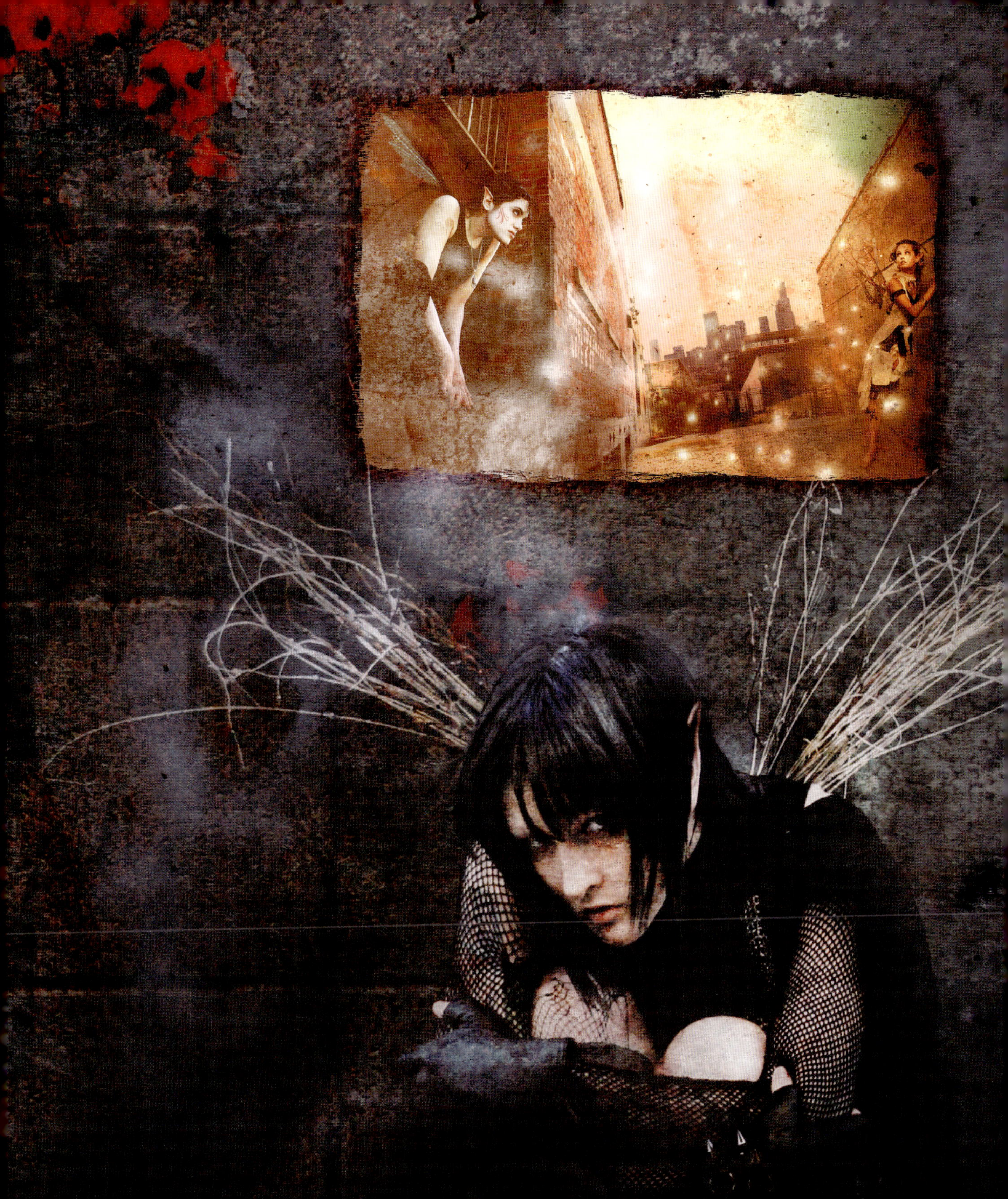

SAD AND CONFUSED, THEY TOOK TO THE STREETS AND ALLEYWAYS IN SEARCH OF SOLACE. THEY HID IN THE UNDERGROUND PLACES, THE ABANDONED PLACES, THE LOST PLACES, OR STALKED STEEL GIRDERS ALONG THE SHARP CORNERS OF BUILDINGS.

It was motion without moving and in these grim places, their wings grew tattered and their light and magic dimmed. They had almost given way to become lost souls selling hope for chance.

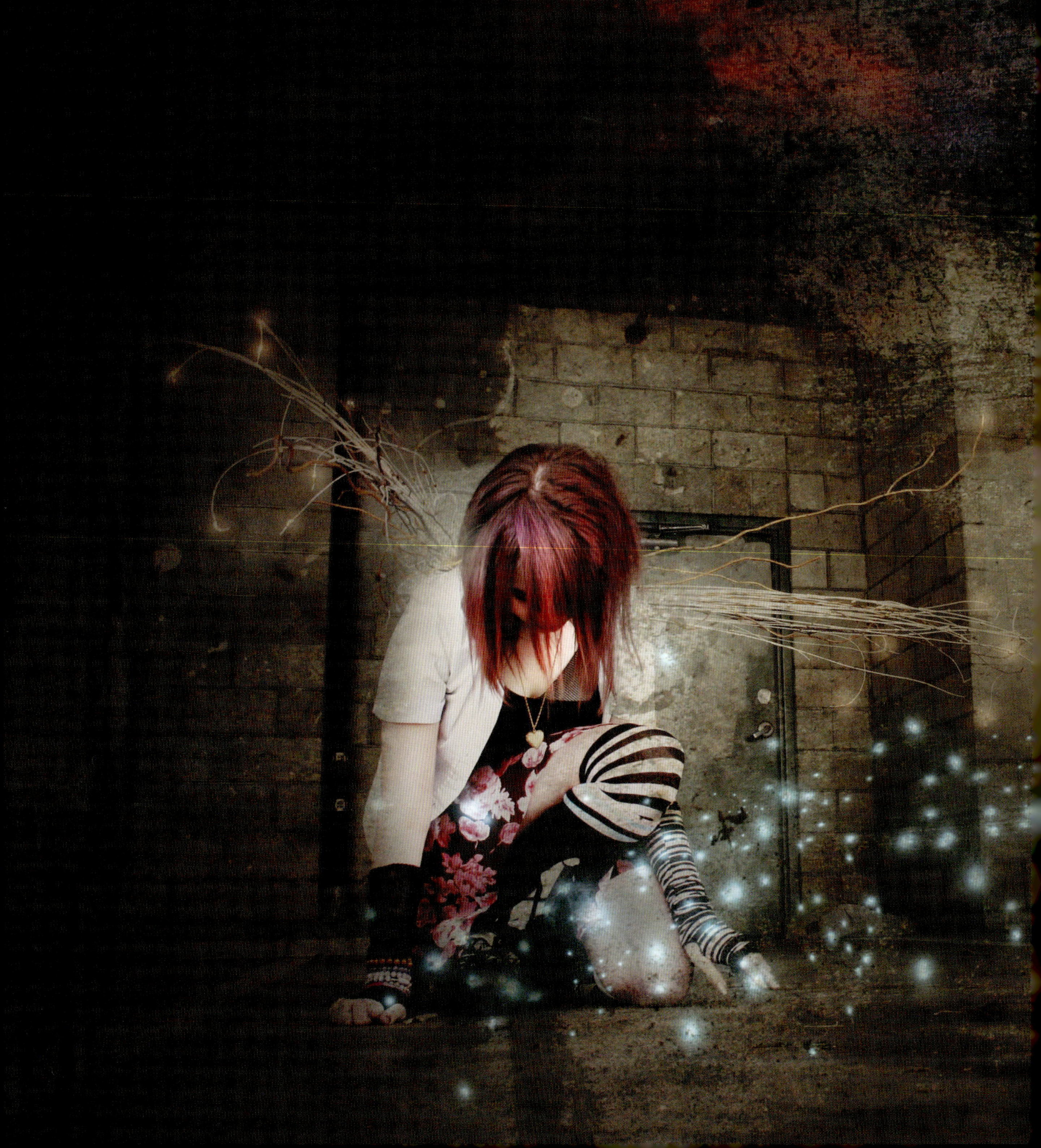

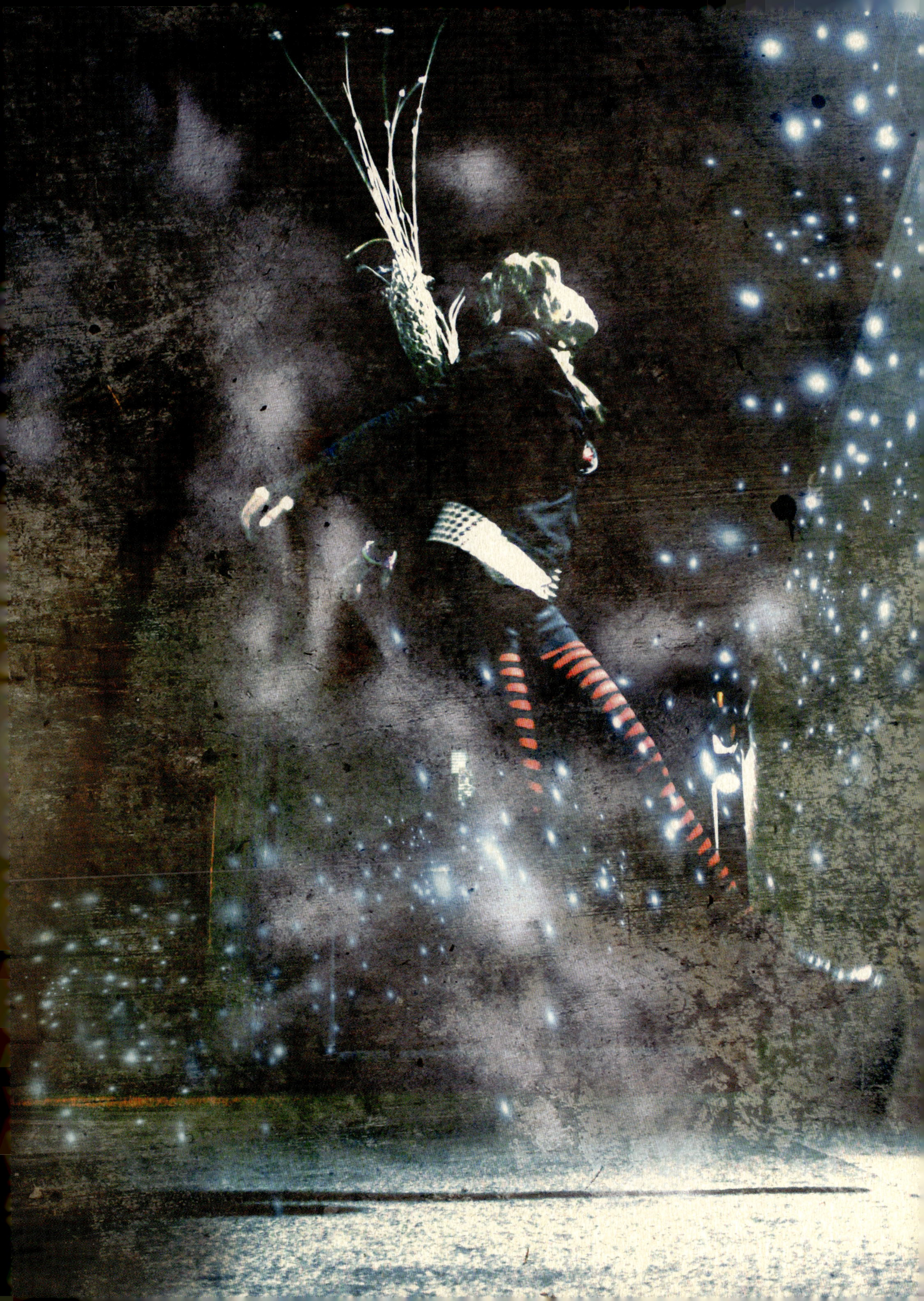

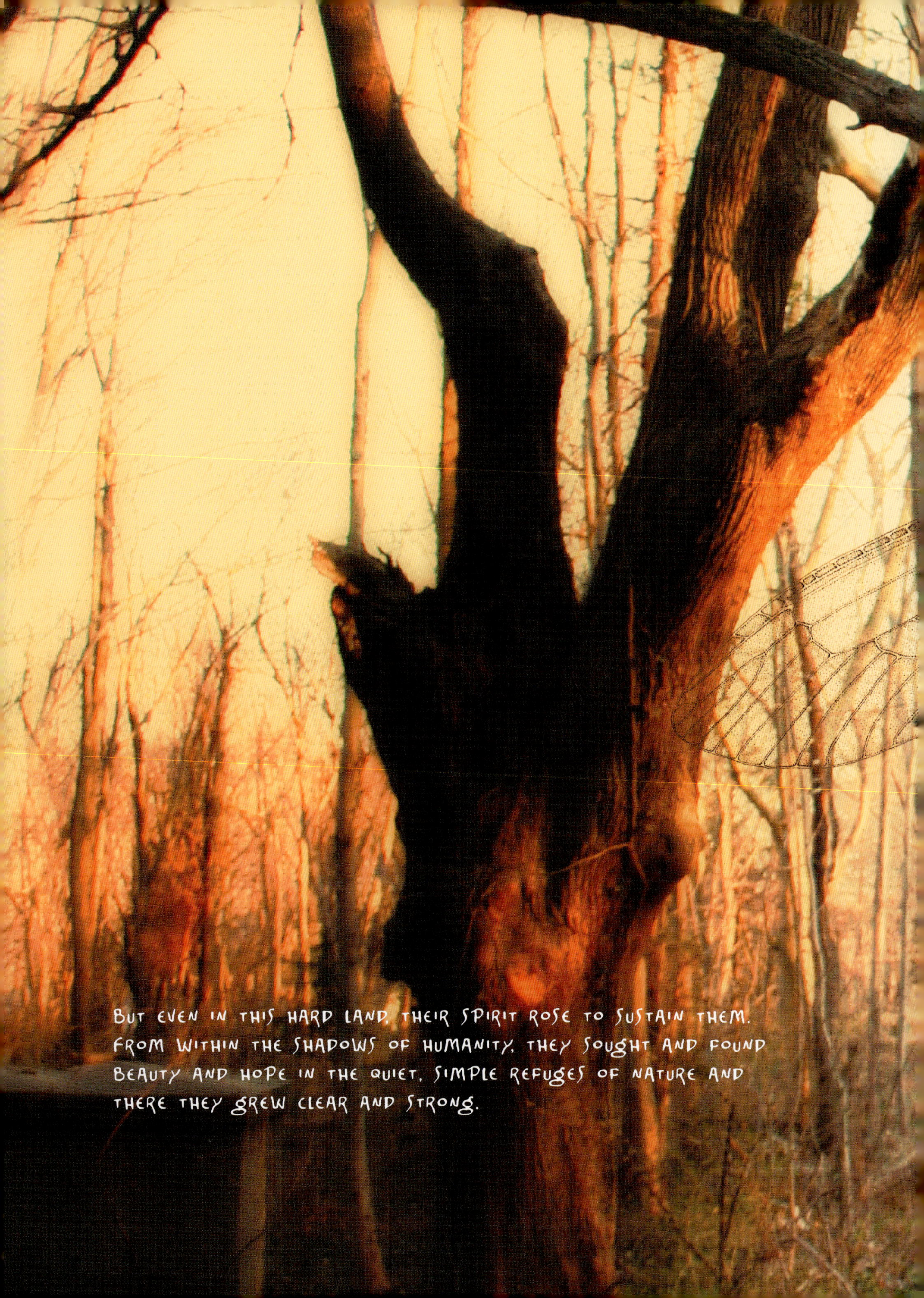

But even in this hard land, their spirit rose to sustain them. From within the shadows of humanity, they sought and found beauty and hope in the quiet, simple refuges of nature and there they grew clear and strong.

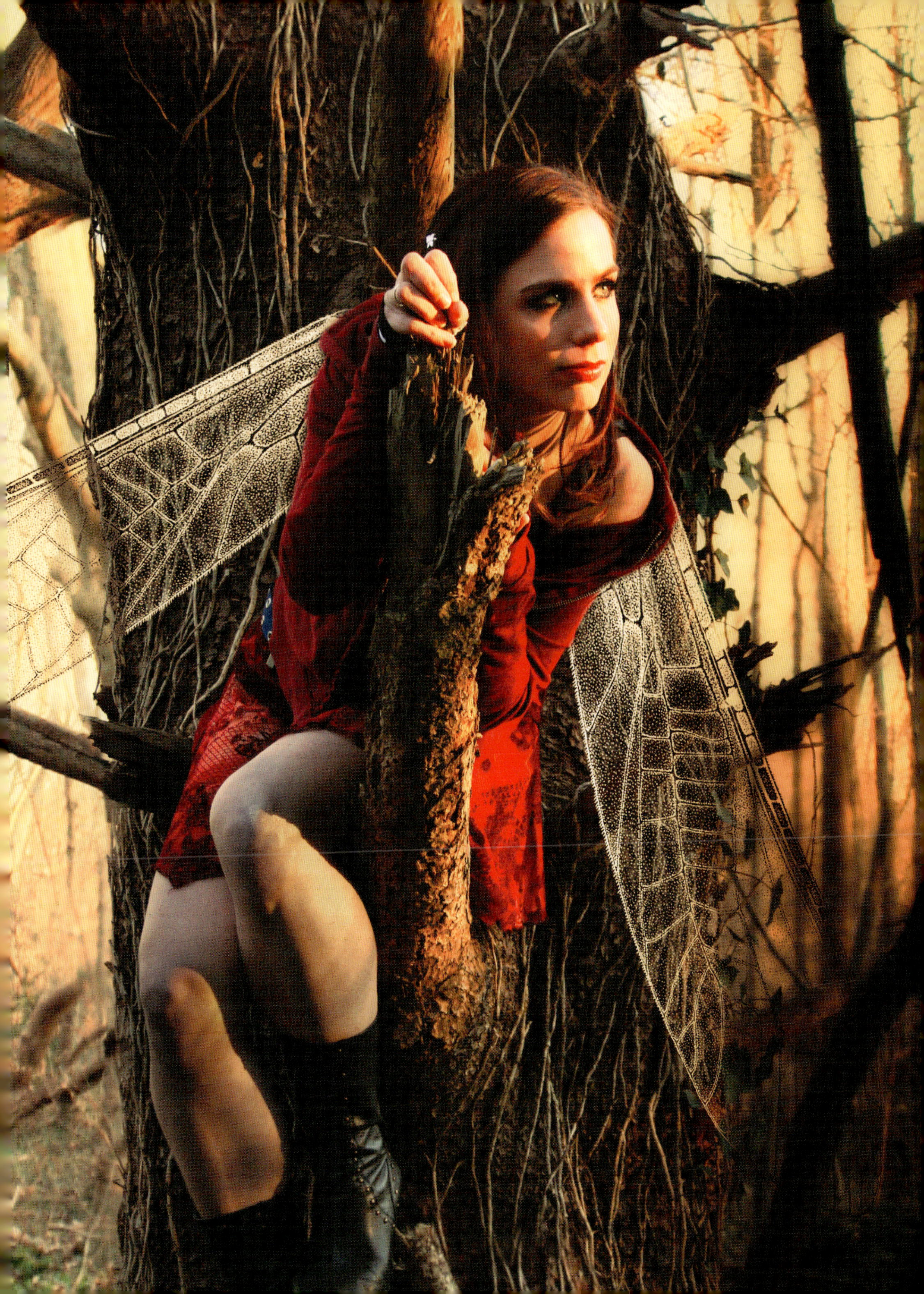

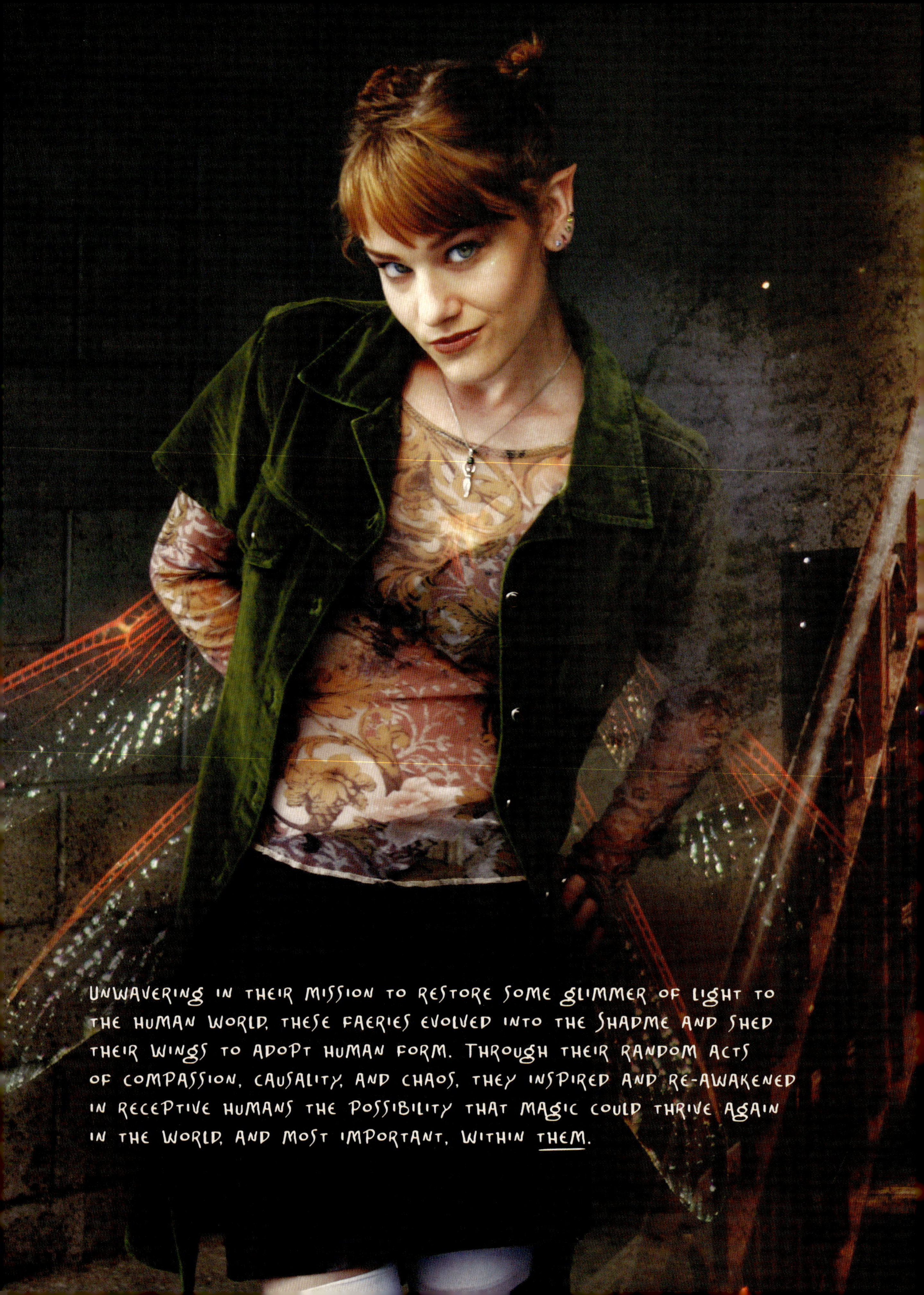

Unwavering in their mission to restore some glimmer of light to the human world, these faeries evolved into the Shadme and shed their wings to adopt human form. Through their random acts of compassion, causality, and chaos, they inspired and re-awakened in receptive humans the possibility that magic could thrive again in the world, and most important, within <u>them</u>.

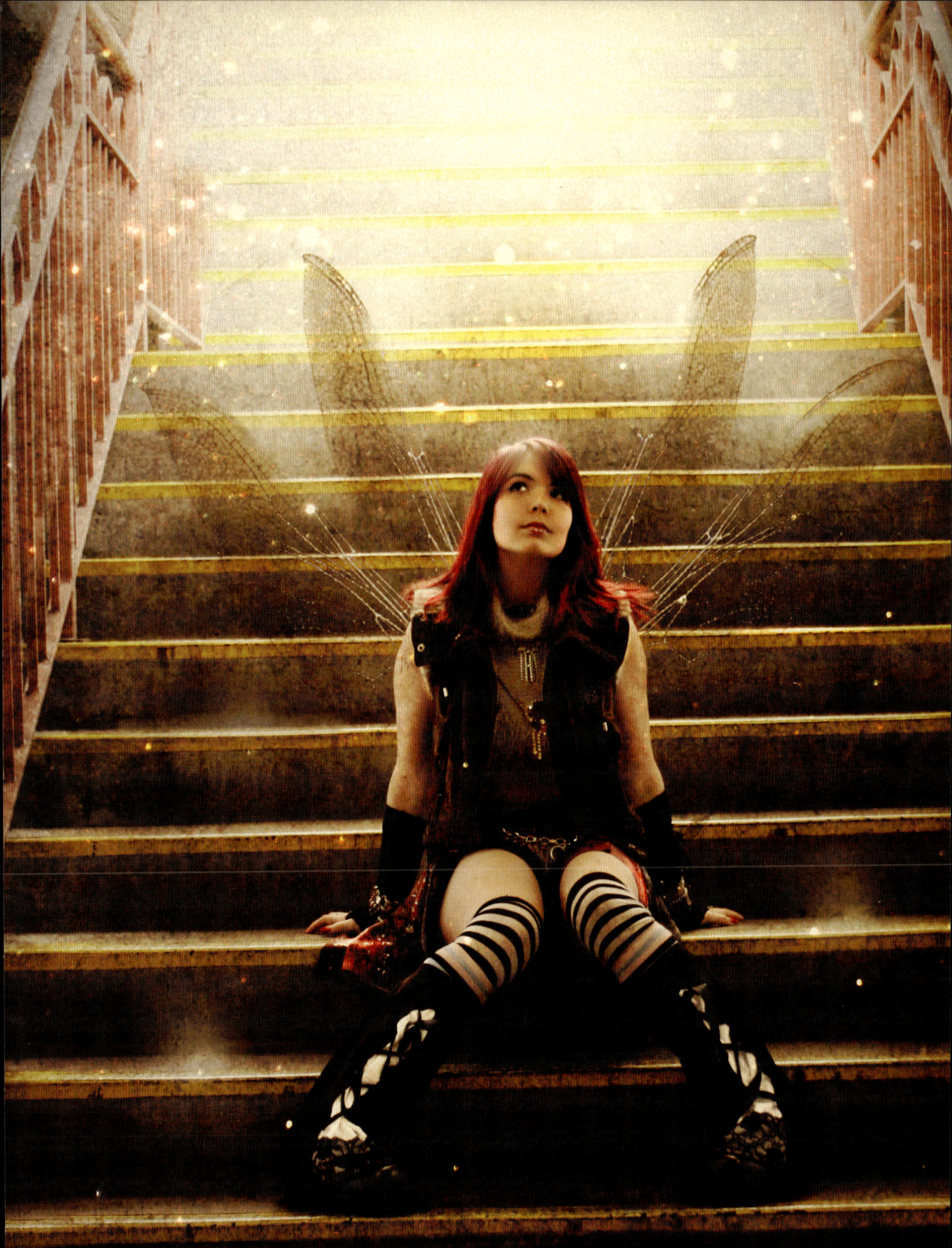

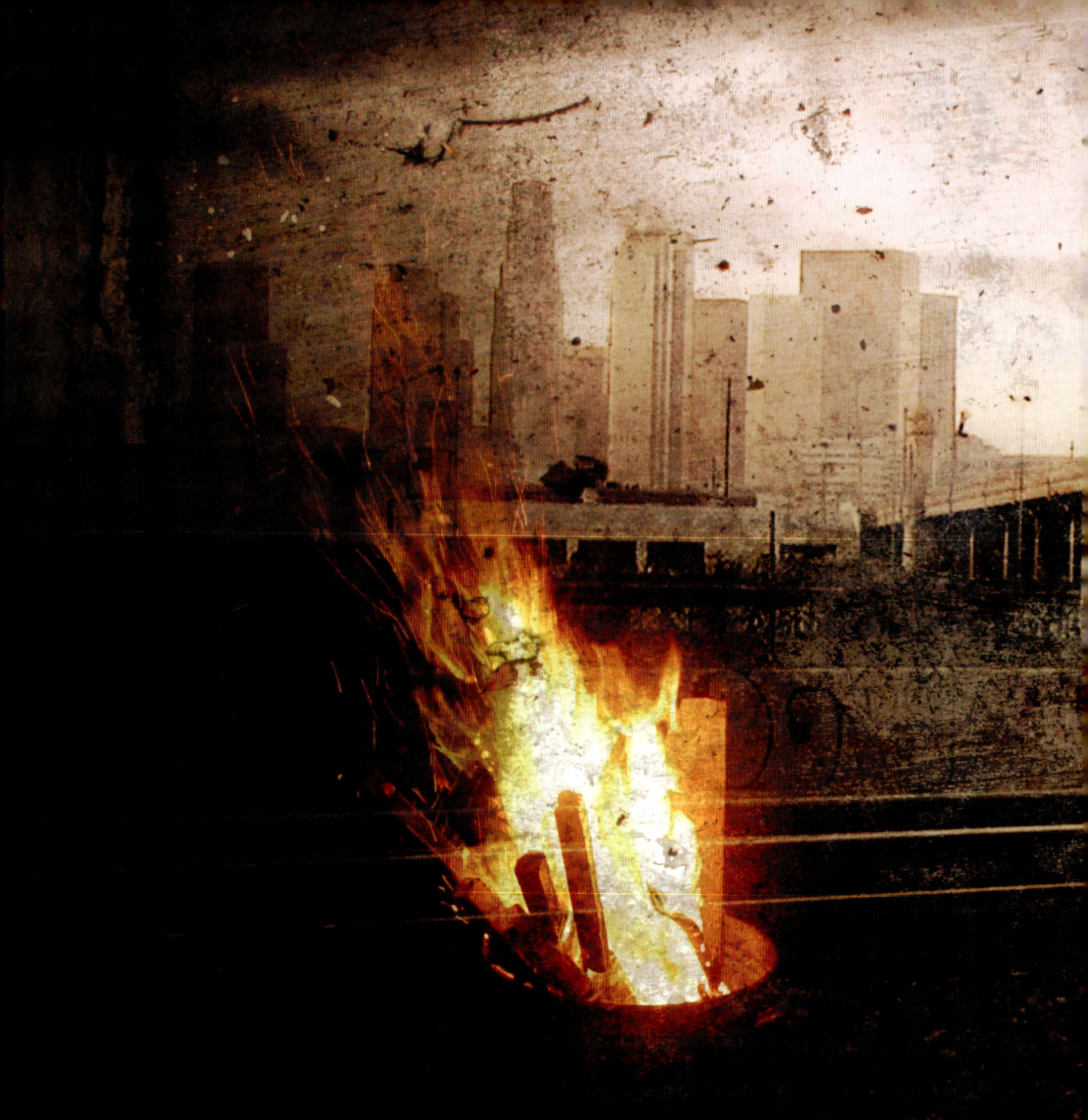

AS THESE SHADME SPARKS IGNITED HOPE, SOME OF THE ANGELS SAW THE EMERGING LIGHT AND COULD NOT IGNORE THE CALL FROM DEEP WITHIN THEM. REBELLIOUSLY THEY PLUMMETED FROM E'VEN LIKE GREAT WHITE BIRDS, SEEN AND UNSEEN, AND AS THEY DID, THEIR WINGS TURNED TO ASH AND THEY BECAME NEPHILIM. TRAPPED IN HUMAN FORM WITH LITTLE OR NO MEMORY OF WHO THEY ONCE HAD BEEN; THE PRICE OF THEIR CHOICE LAID DOWN FROM THEIR KIN IN E'VEN.

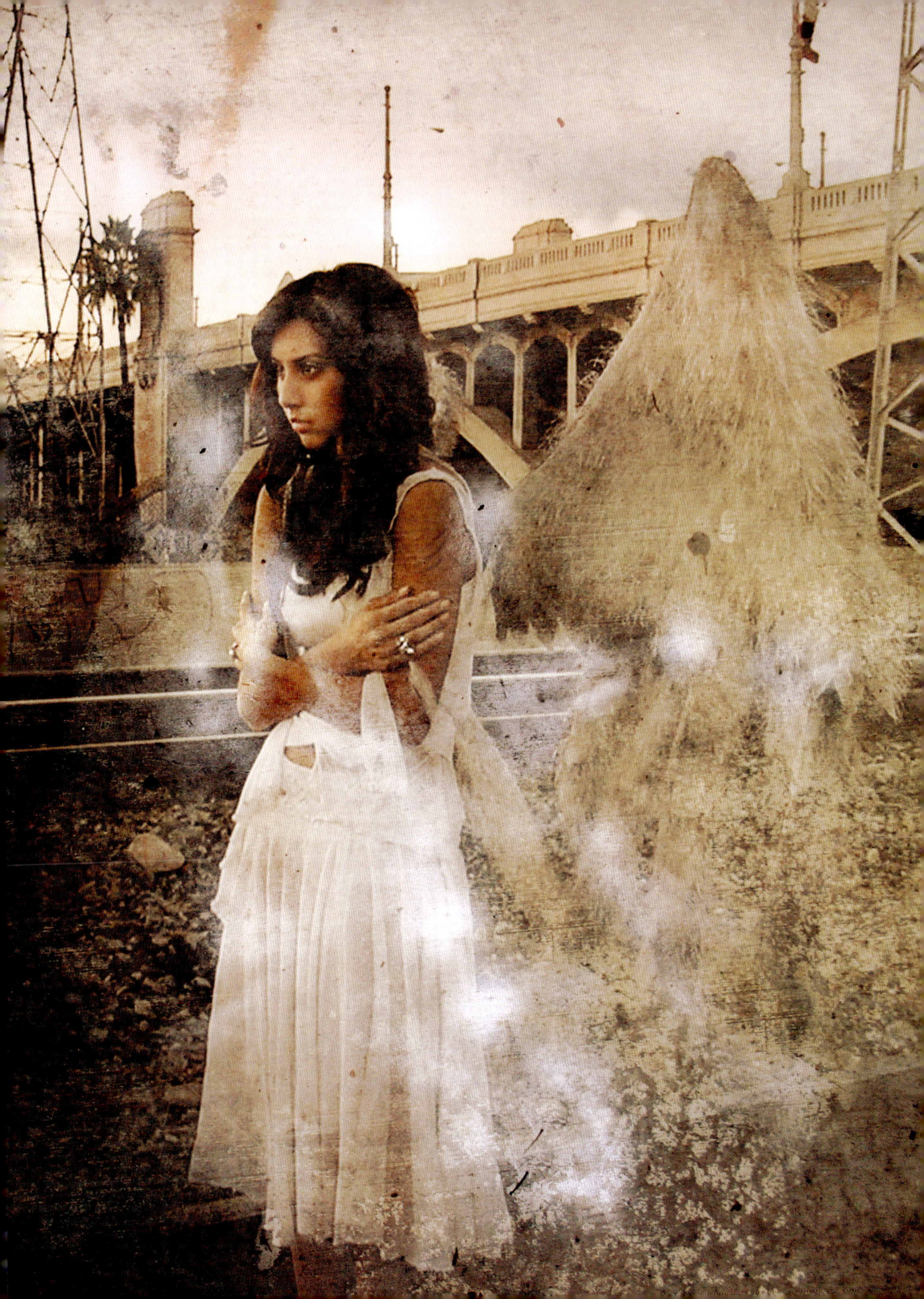

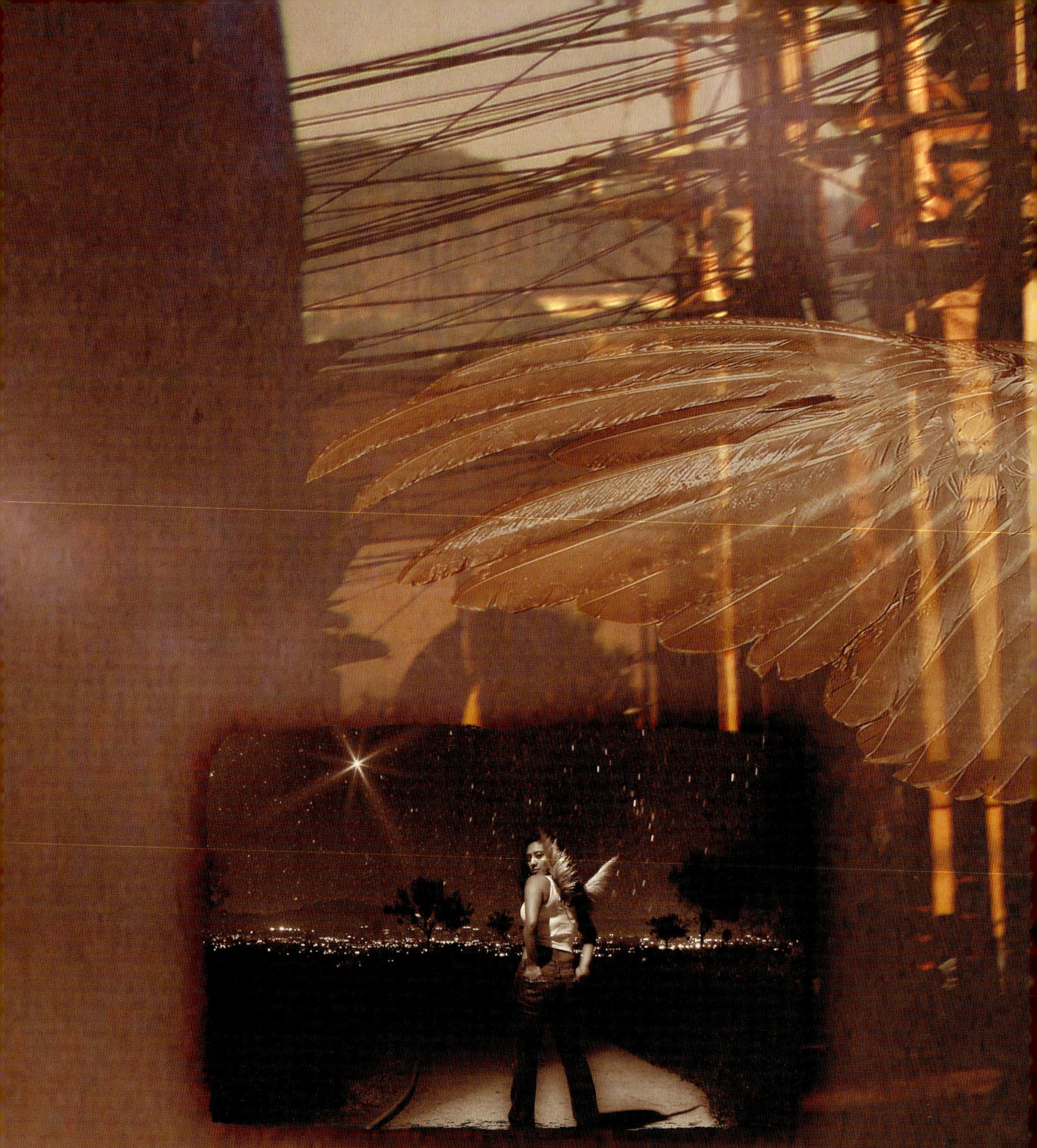

THEY WERE CREATURES OF MIXED ANGEL AND HUMAN BLOOD WHO SUFFERED FROM BOTH NIGHTMARES AND ECSTATIC VISIONS THAT THE HUMAN PART OF THEIR MINDS COULD NOT COMPREHEND AS DEEP DOWN INSIDE THEIR FAERIE NATURE BURNED.

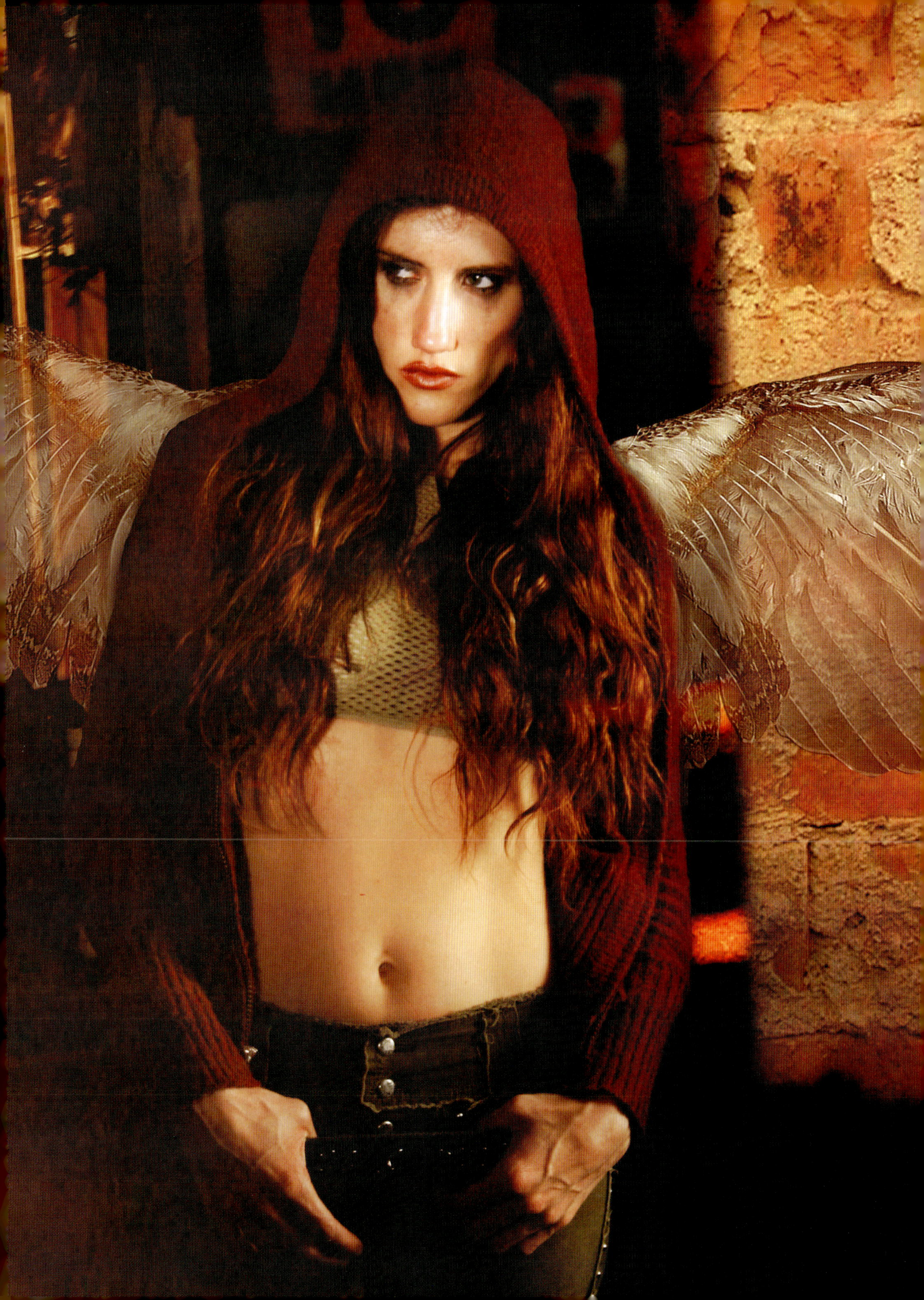

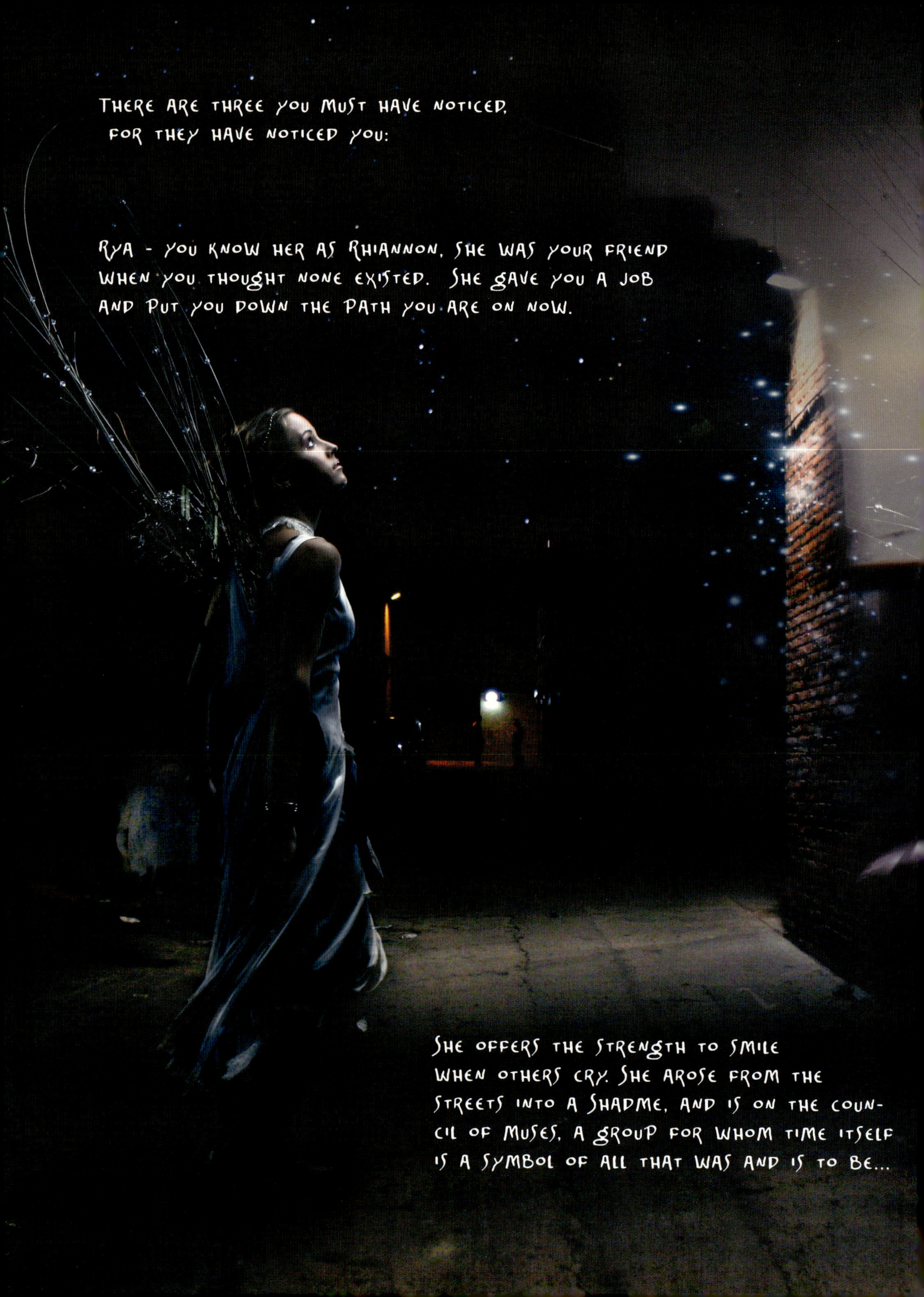

There are three you must have noticed, for they have noticed you:

Rya - you know her as Rhiannon. She was your friend when you thought none existed. She gave you a job and put you down the path you are on now.

She offers the strength to smile when others cry. She arose from the streets into a Shadme, and is on the council of Muses, a group for whom time itself is a symbol of all that was and is to be...

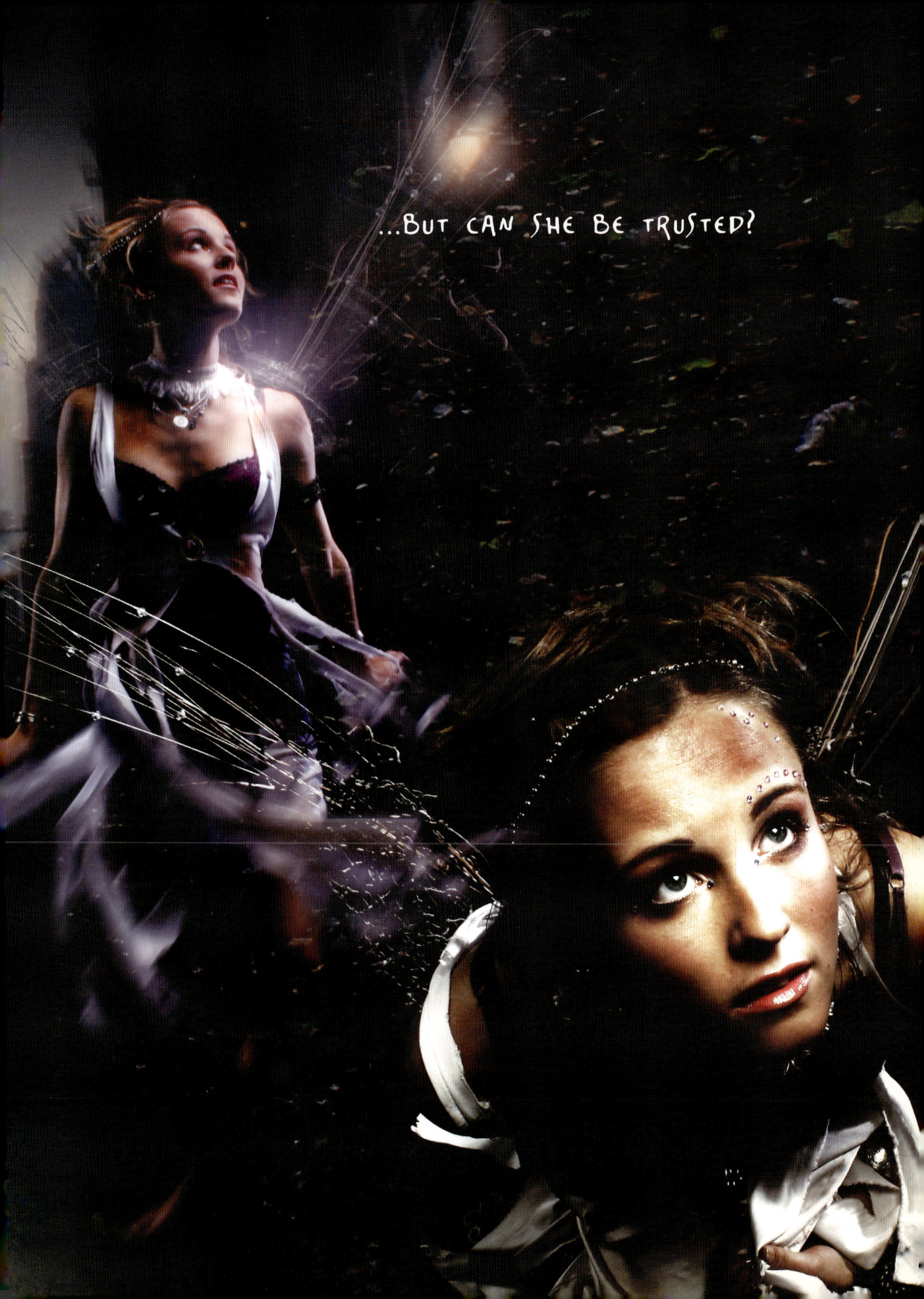
...BUT CAN SHE BE TRUSTED?

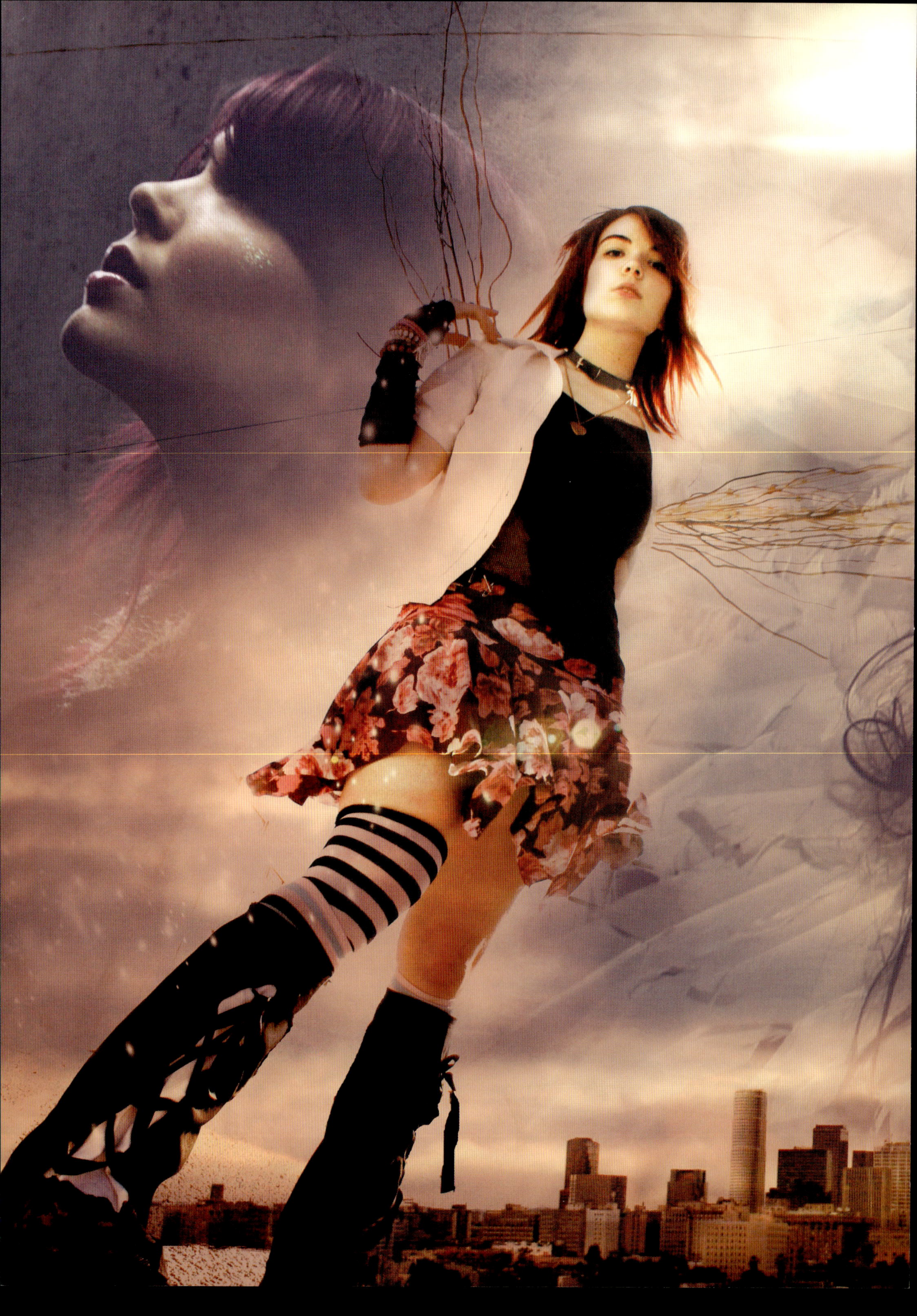

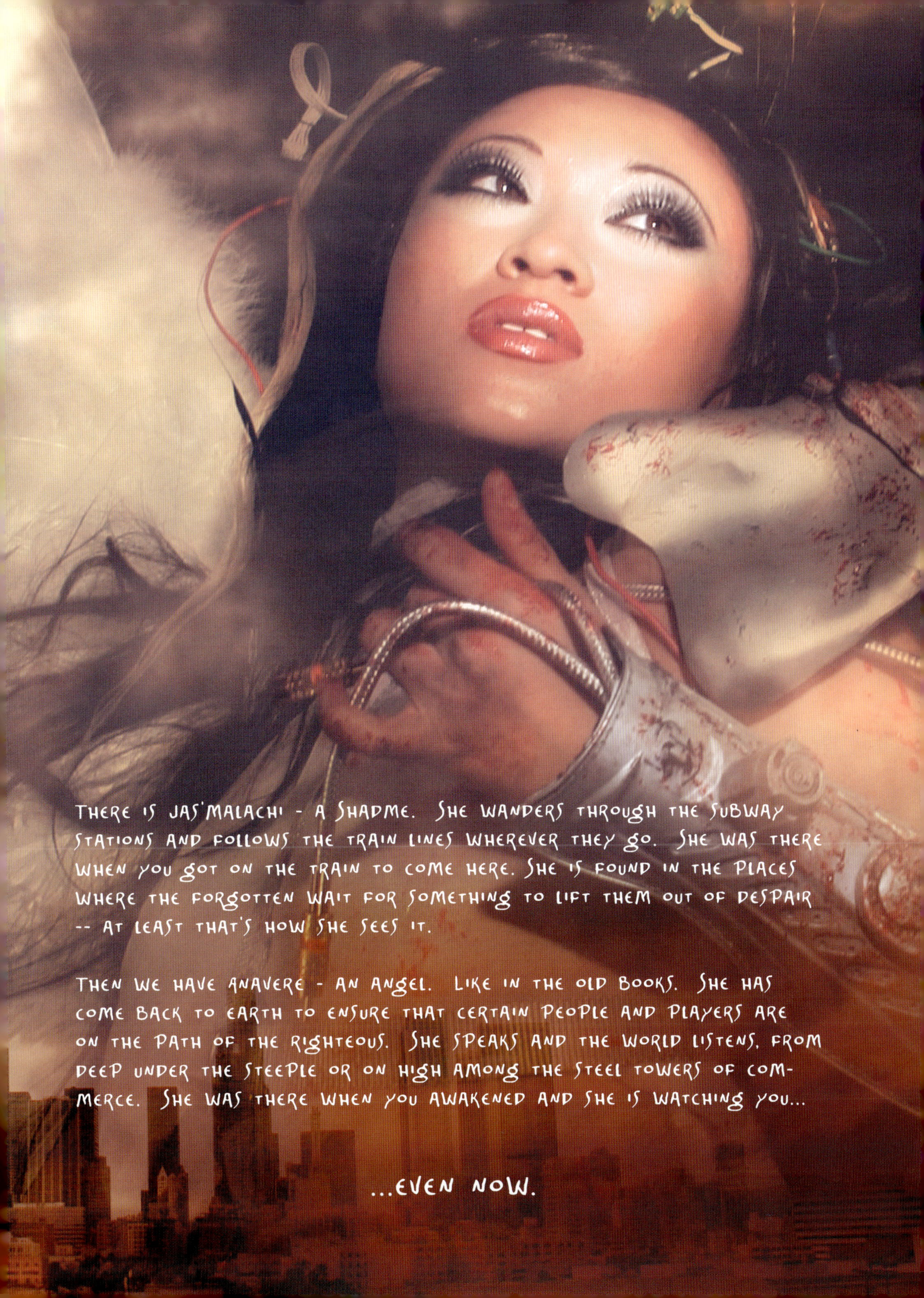

There is Jas'Malachi - a Shadme. She wanders through the subway stations and follows the train lines wherever they go. She was there when you got on the train to come here. She is found in the places where the forgotten wait for something to lift them out of despair -- at least that's how she sees it.

Then we have Anavere - an Angel. Like in the old books. She has come back to earth to ensure that certain people and players are on the path of the righteous. She speaks and the world listens, from deep under the steeple or on high among the steel towers of commerce. She was there when you awakened and she is watching you...

...even now.

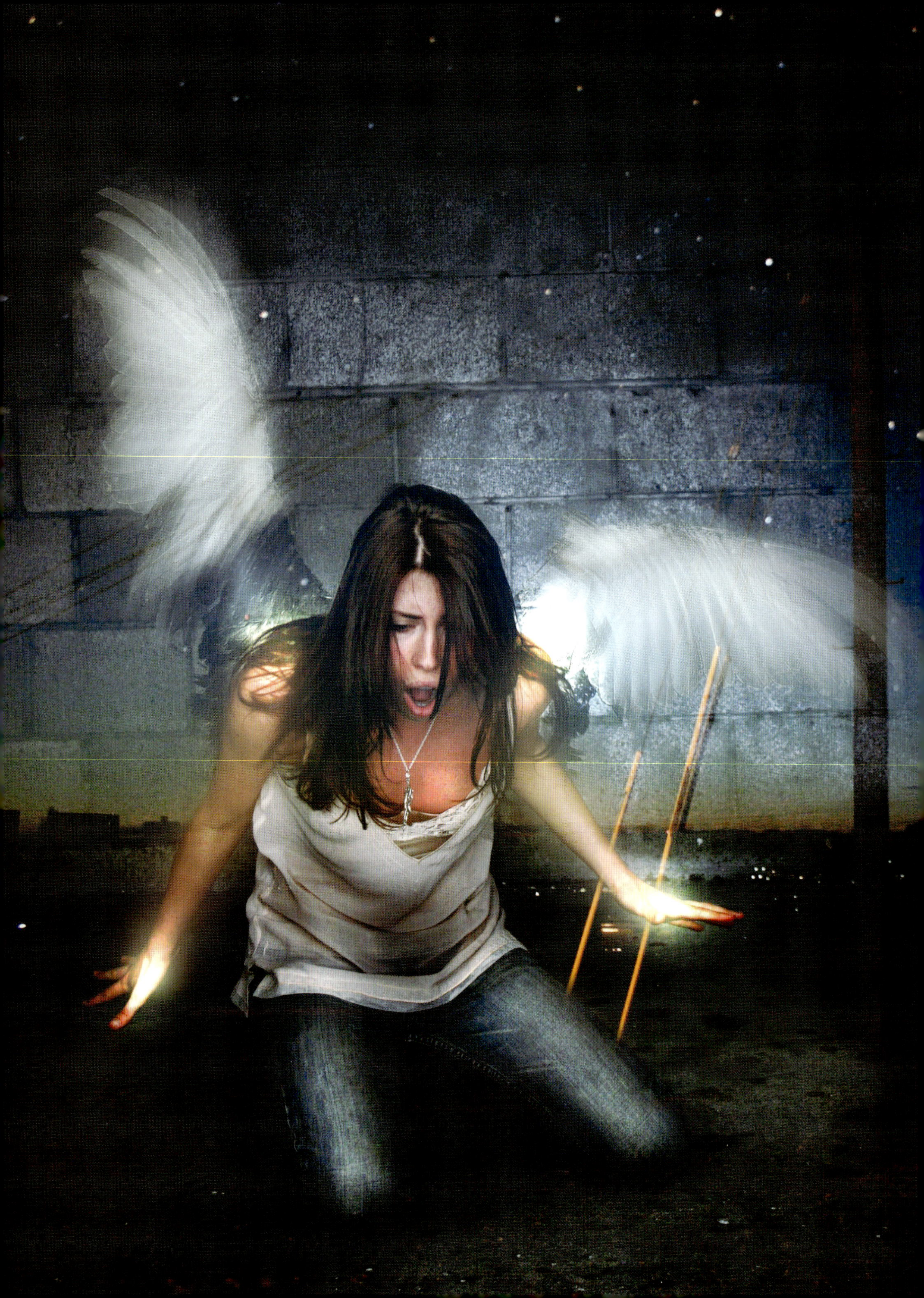

And you of course, are Emily Evans - you have forgotten who you are because you are a nephilim caught between the worlds of faeries and angels. You are hunted by dark things and those who were once dark things. Slowly you awaken to your own powers; I hope you're ready for it. If not, there could be dire consequences. Your reflection may not be seen by the average human but others see you...

...and they are coming.

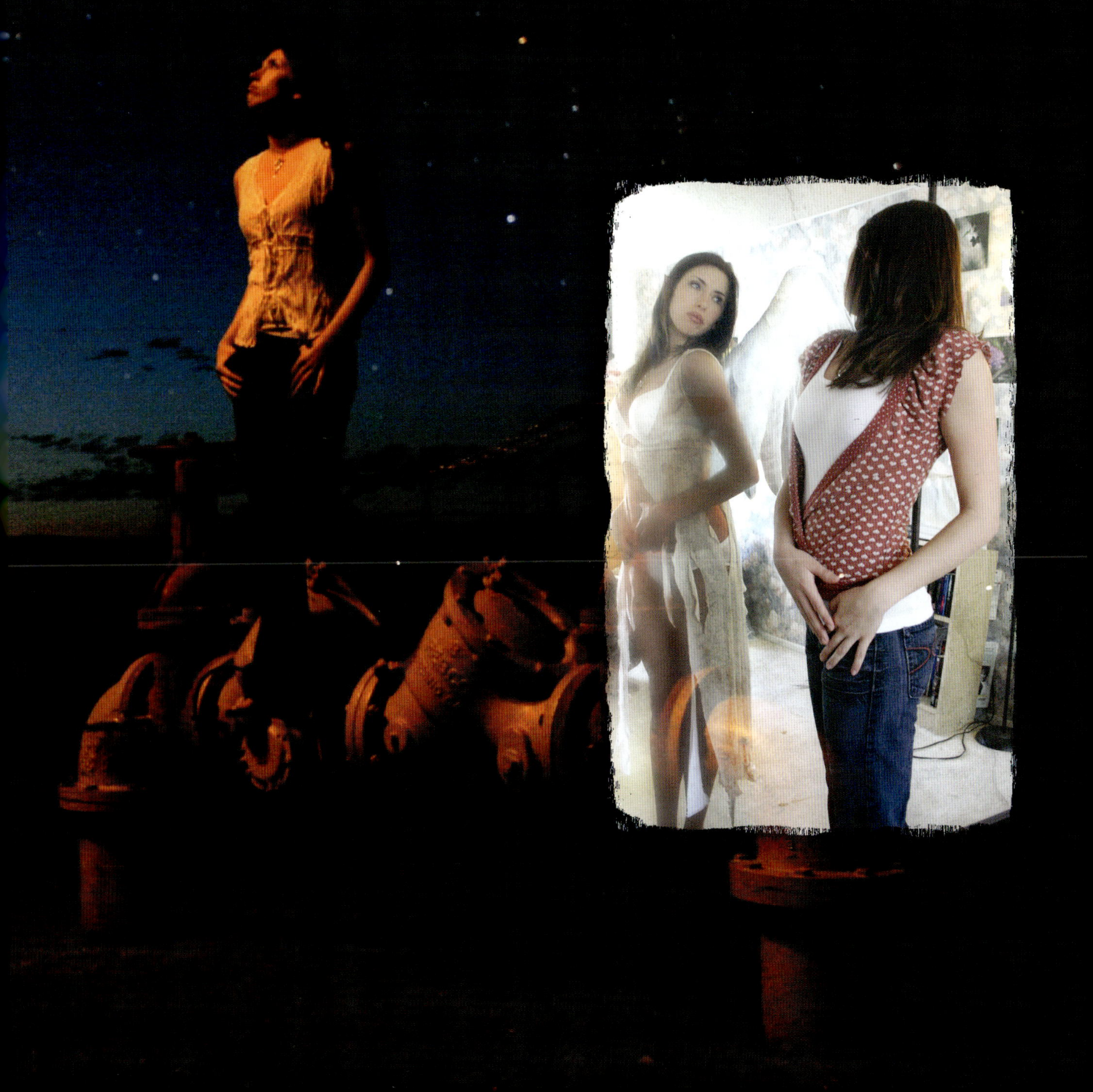

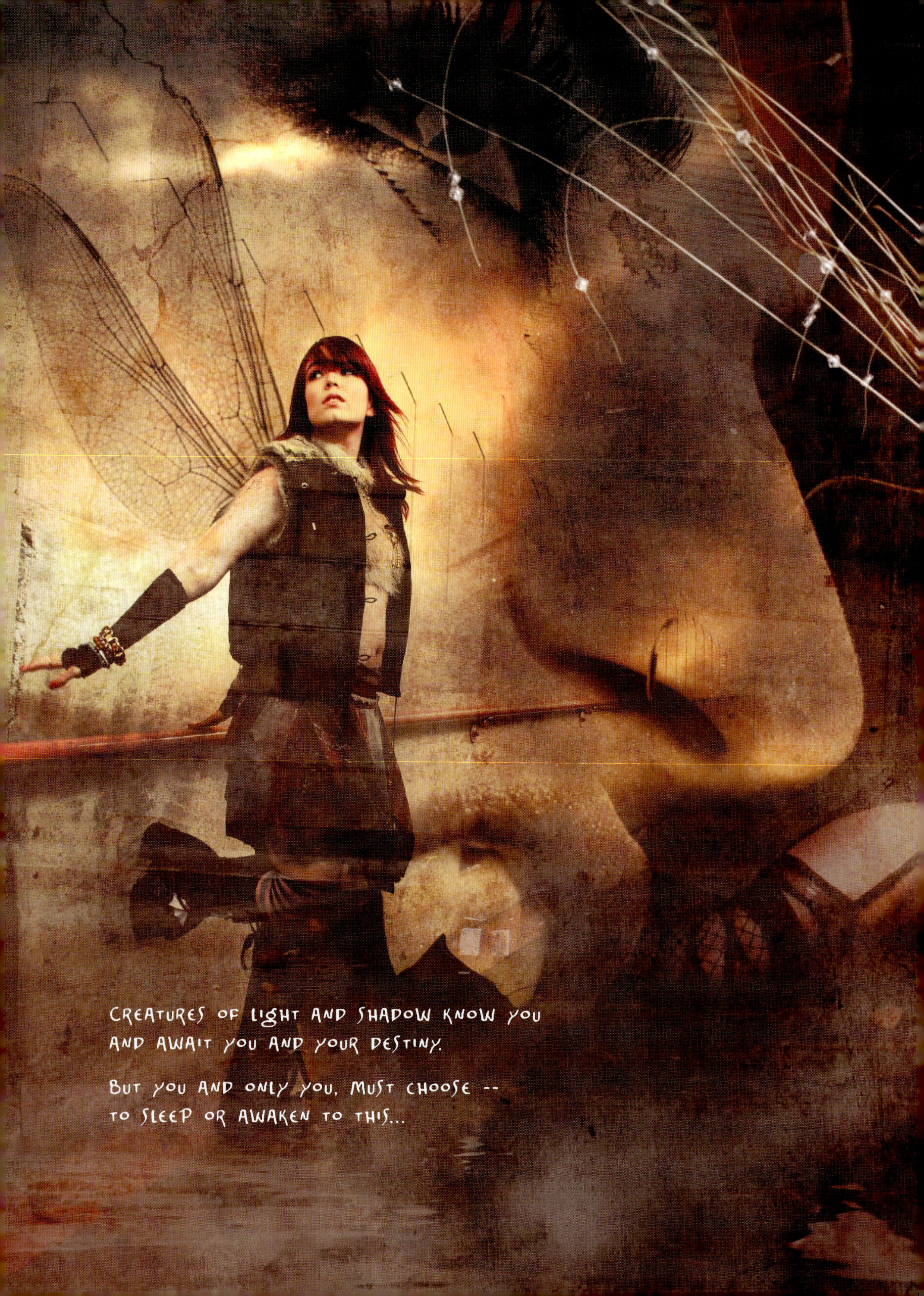
CREATURES OF LIGHT AND SHADOW KNOW YOU
AND AWAIT YOU AND YOUR DESTINY.
BUT YOU AND ONLY YOU, MUST CHOOSE --
TO SLEEP OR AWAKEN TO THIS...

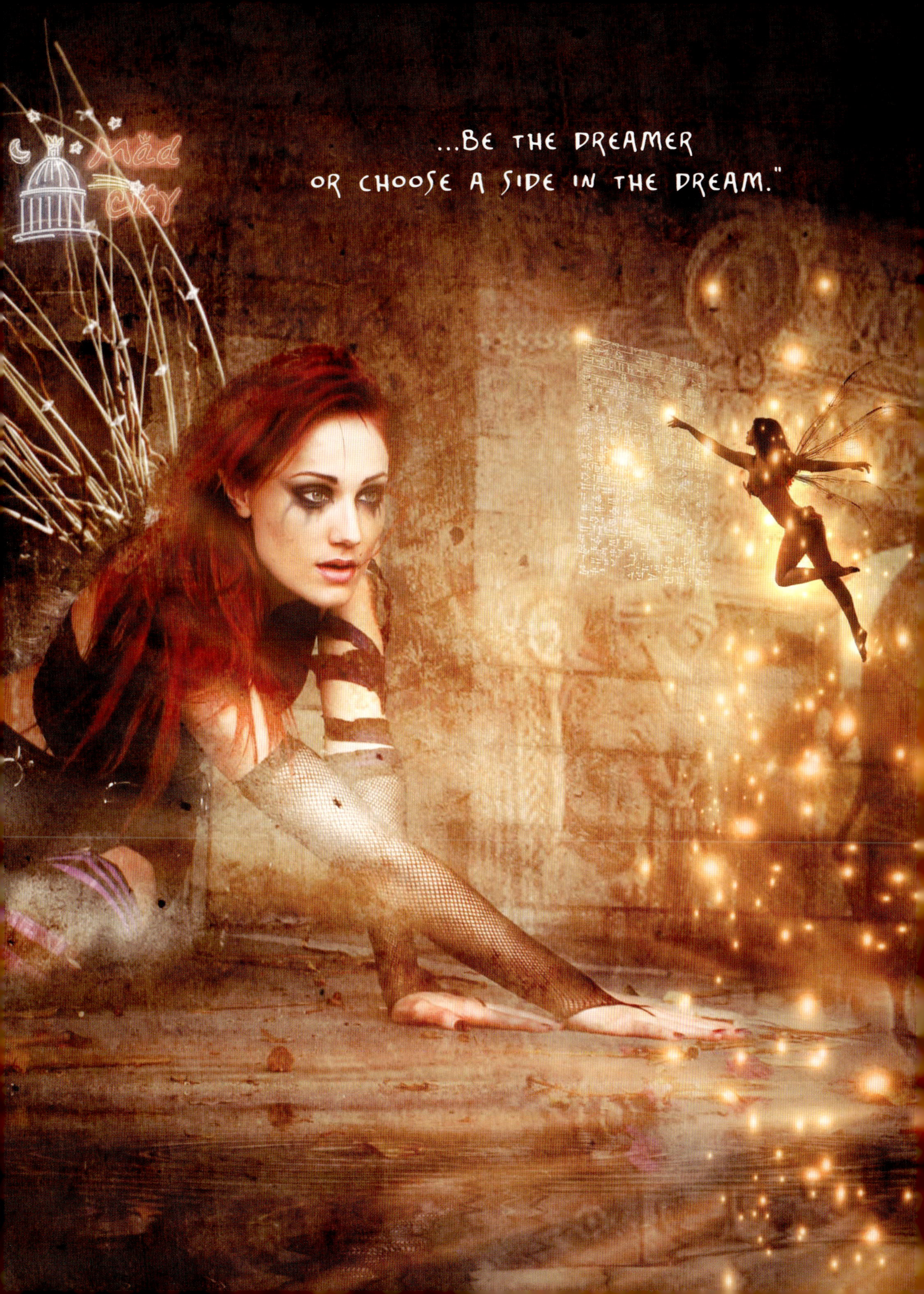
Mad
City
...Be the dreamer
or choose a side in the dream."

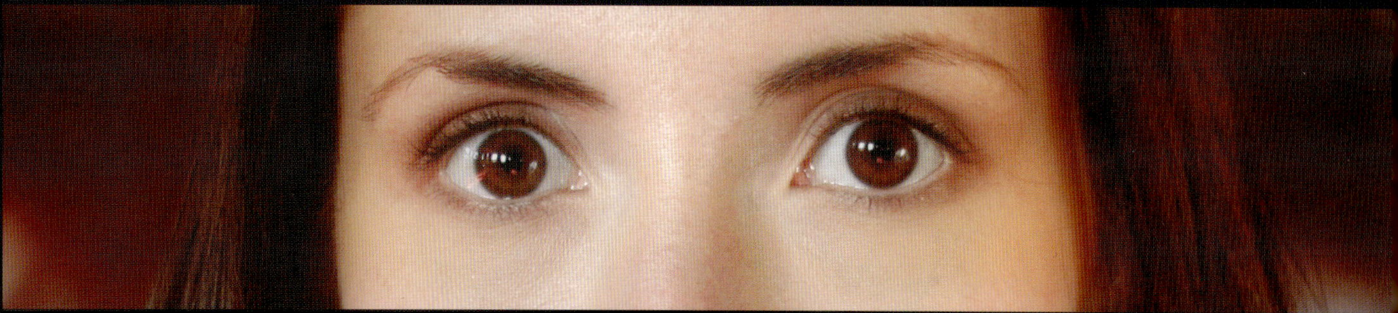

"That's it? Is all that… true?"

"Yes and yes."

I sipped my glass without noticing it was empty. I looked around me, processing this and all I had seen in the last few weeks. "I…"

"So, Ms. Evans, I gave you your truth; now it's time to pay up. We had an agreement."

"Now? I mean, OK, but can't it wait?

I really don't know what I think of all this, I need time."

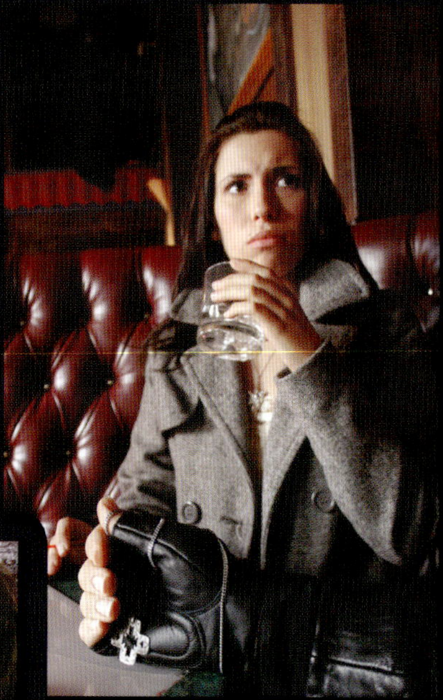

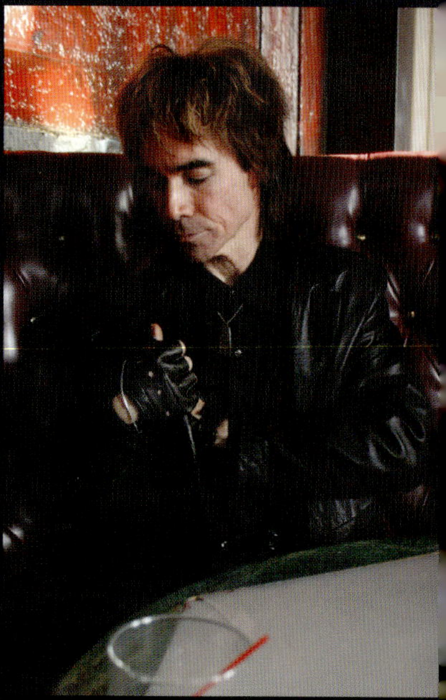

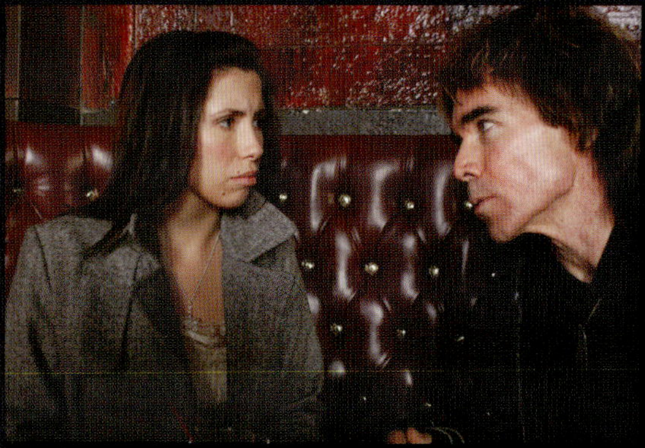

"Sorry, no waiting. As you said, you don't *have* the time. We had a deal, yes?"

"Yes… yes, we did."

I took a deep breath and looked up to him. "OK, let's get it over with. What's the price?"

He took my hands once again and moved them across the table.

Three cards lay before me.

I looked up and I was lost in his ancient eyes as I heard the faraway voice say:

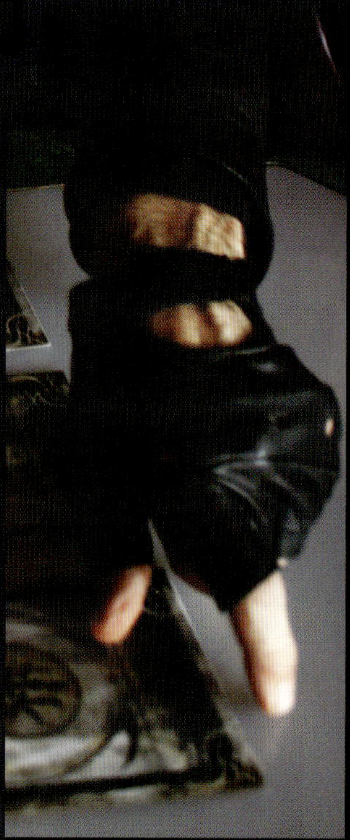

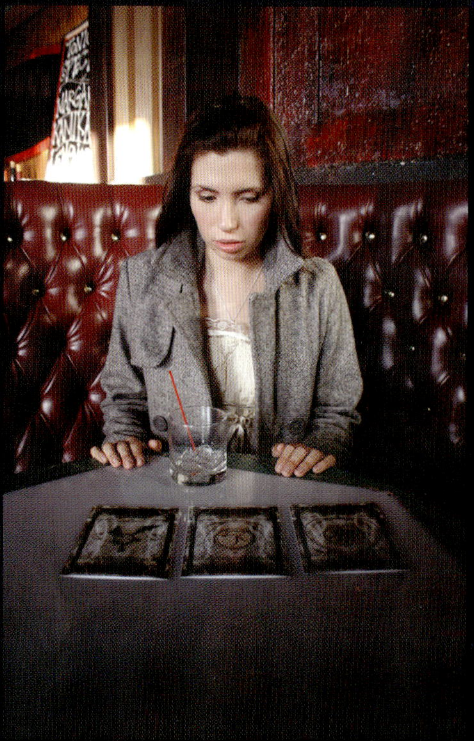

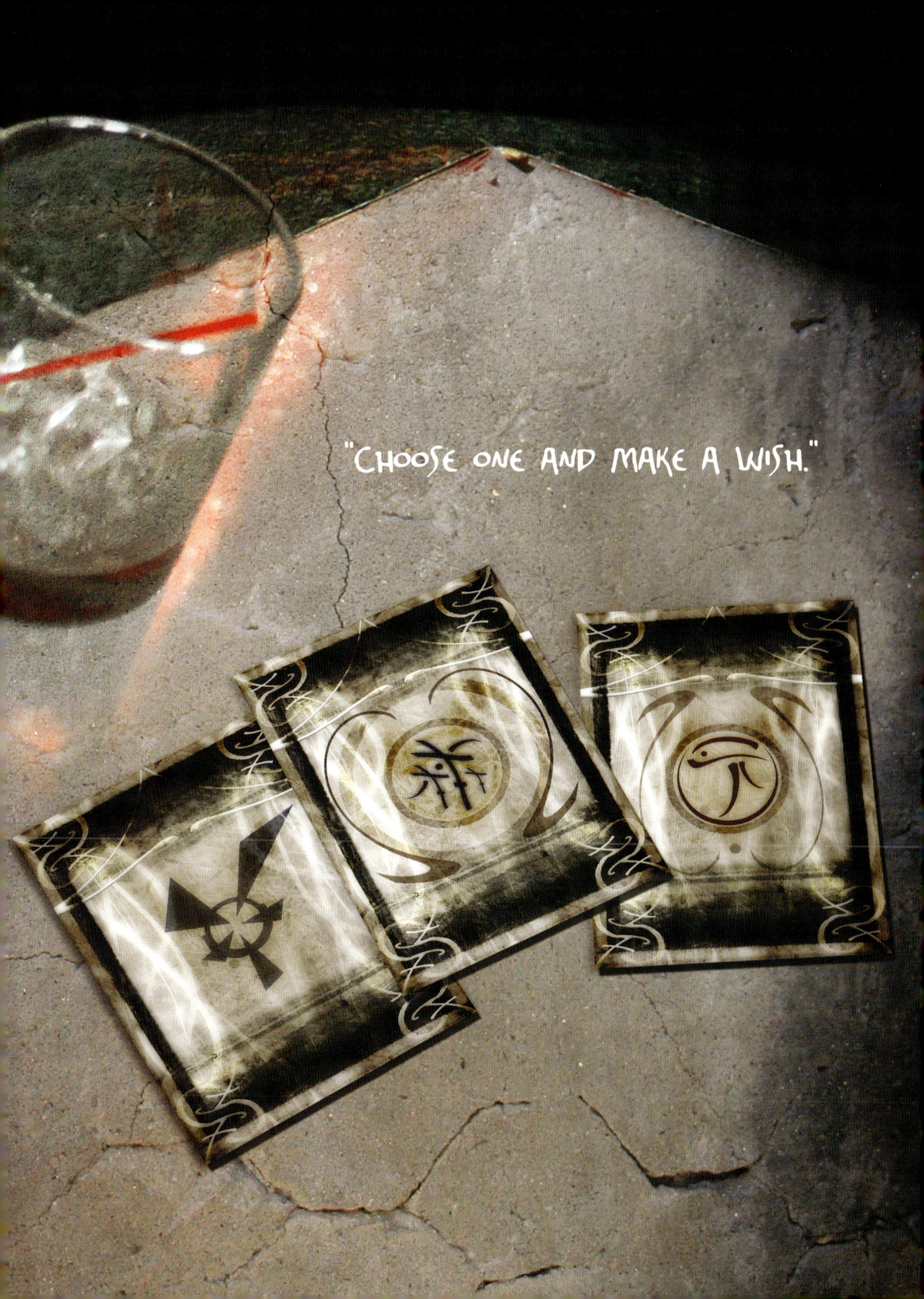
"CHOOSE ONE AND MAKE A WISH."

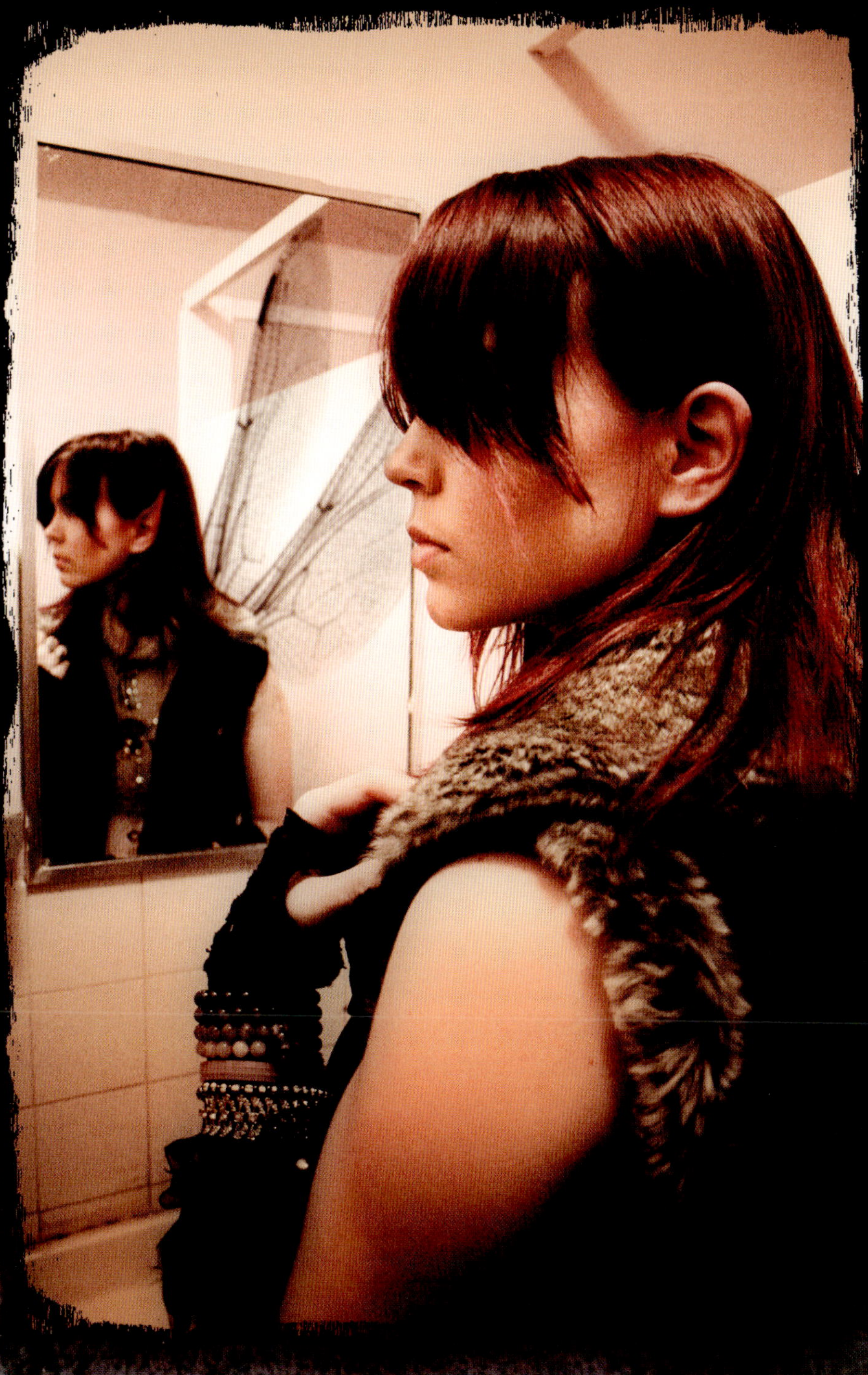

DEDICATION:

For Donny, the supportive ***true believer*** who understood it didn't have to be perfect... it just had to work. Feel the Love. Anything can happen.

And to the true ***Shadme*** of the world,

Motion and Passion Eternal.

Tah Sage Aseala!

CREDITS:

Story & Photography: J. Corsentino

Muses (in order of appearance):

Sara E.R. Fletcher, Amy Short, Elizabeth Maxwell, Gar Robertson, Kristen Marie, Sarah Day, Lacey Cava, Sunny Subramanian, Teresa Hagen, Erin Layne, Celia Palomino, Natasha Moufavej, Meaghan Cronin, Vivian, Yaya Han, Raluca Iorga, Apryl Faye, Lisa Goodwin, Amy Barklow, Luz Flores, Lauren Smith, Melodie Gore, Shinya, Theresa Donneley, Mahdis, Natalya Bryant, Jenelle Perez, & Juliya Chernetsky

Make up Artist: Andrea Dow

Guest Make-up Artists: Cole Saad, Michelle Deiti, Julie Michelle, Kelli Andresen, Lauren Smith, Zebek, Eddie Inda

Stylists: Donny Ha & J. Corsentino

Guest Stylists: Lisa Goodwin, Yaya Han, Shinya, Vanessa Zuloaga

VERY SPECIAL THANKS TO:

Donny (you make me happy when skies are GREY), Lauren (for sheltering me during the AI storm with Froud and Faeries), Andrea (for painting more naked bodies than originally intended), Maxwell (for waiting while we found a parking space). Sara Fletcher (for a constant reminder of what a faerie is), Nathan (for the constant access to your building), Luz (for kidnapping me several times during this project), Laura Lightfine (for memories... for France... for dreams... for Stephen Jenkins and all the Mesopotamian cow gods). Peter Cancilla ("More misadventures?" "Adventures, old friend!"), Amy Raasch (still livin' the dream), Gar-man (for keeping my wine and spare moments chill), Jordan Elgrably (for the time and space), and Nial Kane (for the drinks and discounts that kept the nights & ideas flowing). Our Friends at Faerie Chronicles: Margaret Dean (who lit the fire under our collective arses), David Windham (entil zah), and Tracey Cornett (for letting me cheat at War). Mankind is Obsolete (for keeping the music and insanity at high levels), Robert Gould (for the discovery), Stephanie Lostimolo (for her design and company at Comicon), East Coast Camera (35mm wasn't the same after I left), Nancy Berman (for her words), and the original Faerie visionary, Brian Froud (for keeping all our imaginations active).

And to my Parents Marie & Peter

(sorry for the mess -- metaphorically, metaphysically, & literally.)

For further credit details go to ***timeofthefaeries.com/credits.html***

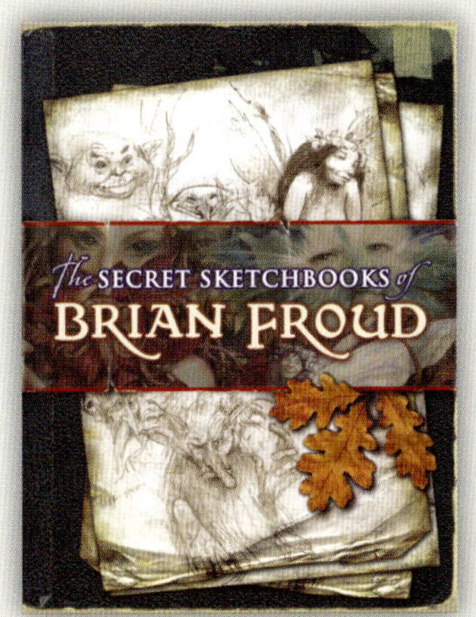

The Seceret Sketchbook of
Brian Froud

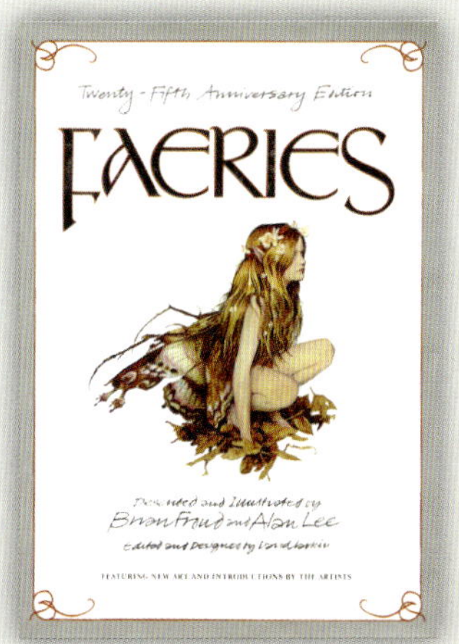

Faeries: 25th Anniversary
Edition

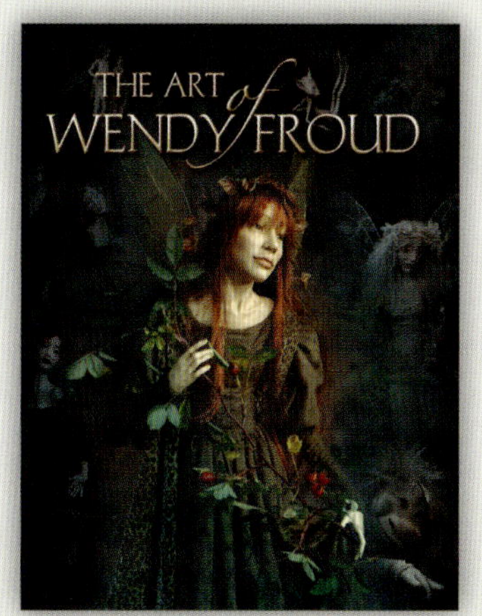

The Art of
Wendy Froud

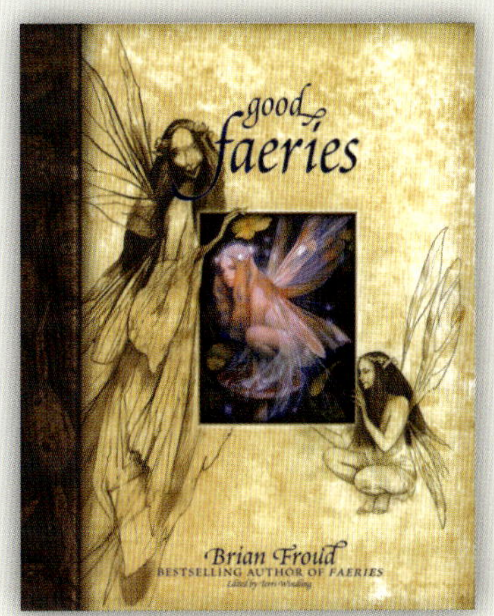

Good Faeries / Bad Faeries

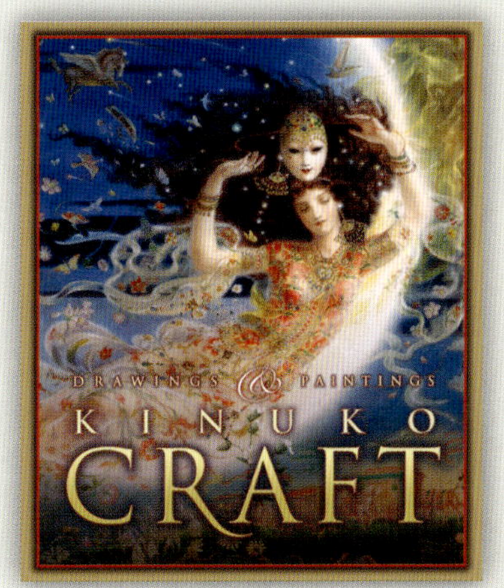

Kinuko Craft:
Drawings & Paintings

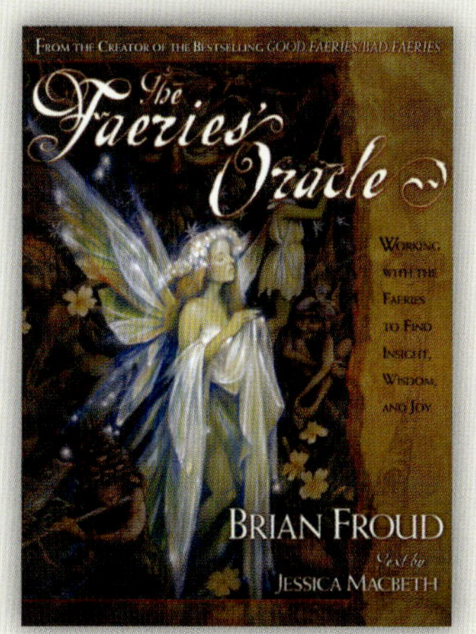

The Faeries' Oracle

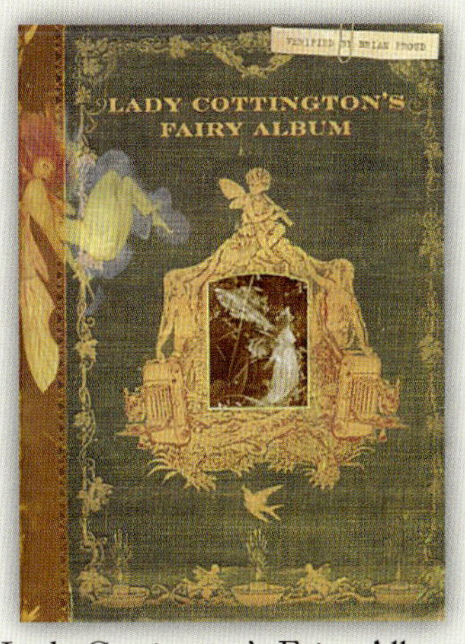

Lady Cottington's Fairy Album

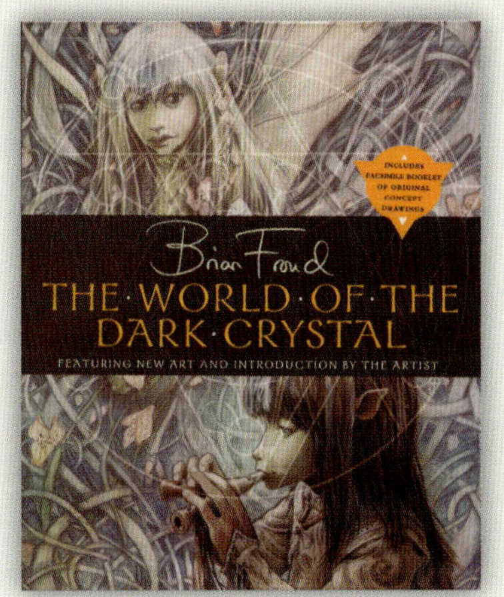

The World of the Dark Crystal

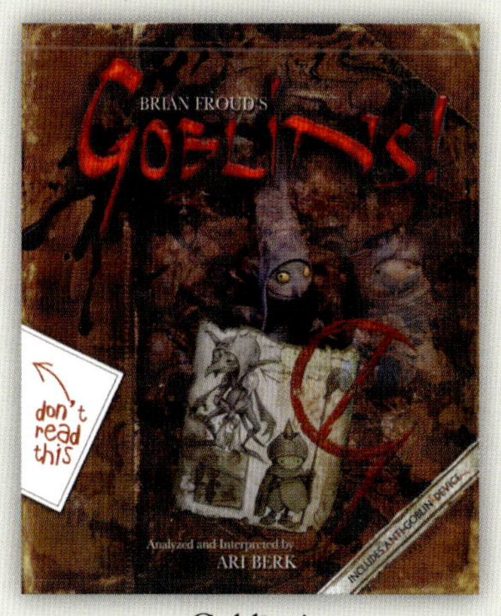

Goblins!

Available wherever books are sold, and at:
imaginosis.com

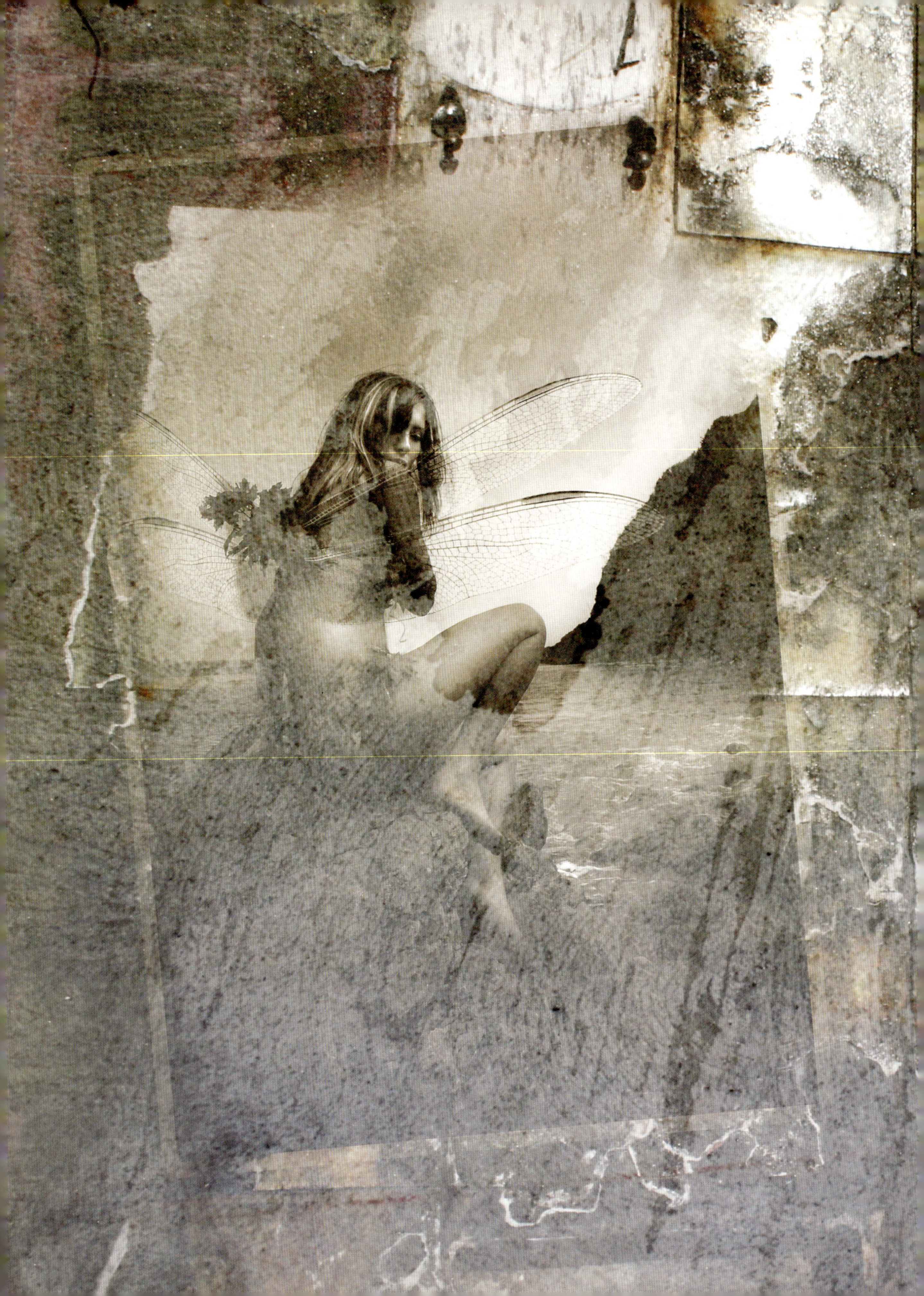

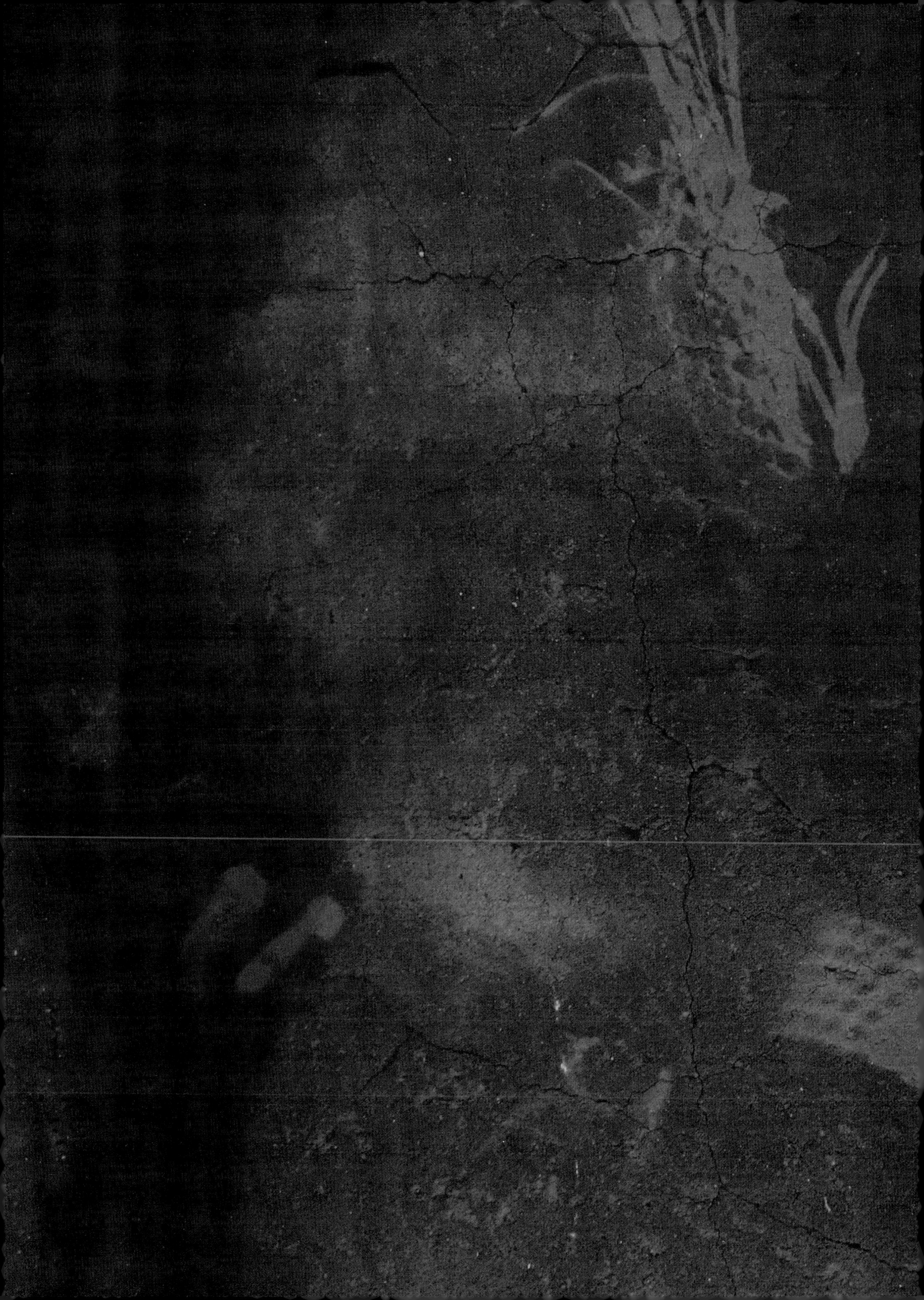

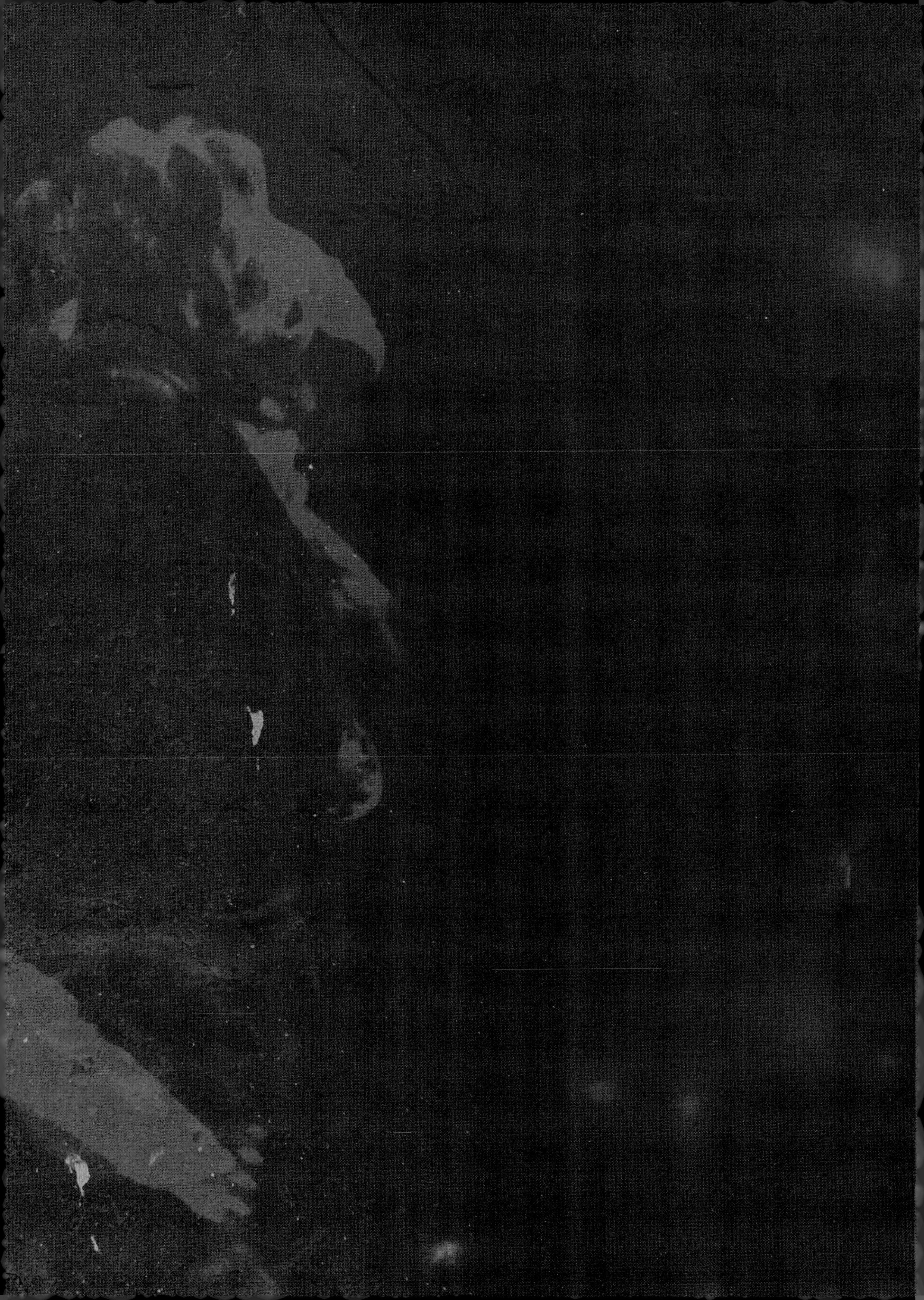